COOKING OVER THREE GENERATIONS

THE GERMAN HERITAGE

THE SAN FRANCISCO INFLUENCE

AND THEN THERE IS ME!

RECIPES ORIGINATED, COLLECTED, OR ALTERED

BY

GLADYS WORDEN CRUM

* * * * * * * * * *

ILLUSTRATED

BY

GLADYS WORDEN CRUM

MURCO MOUNTAIN PUBLISHING
VOLCANO, CALIFORNIA

COOKING OVER THREE GENERATIONS

Published by Murco Mountain Publishing
19582 Mella Drive, Volcano, CA 95689

First Printing: February 1988

Crum, Gladys Worden, 1910-
  Cooking over three generations.

  Includes index.
  1. The German Heritage. 2. The San Francisco Influence. 3. And Then There Is Me!

Library Of Congress Catalog Card Number: 87-62877

  ISBN Number 0-9619654-0-1

641.5

Printed in the United States of America

To Newt, my husband, critic, editor and taster, who has survived the years with a sense of humor, calling himself "the Waist King" and "the Human Garbage Disposal." Without his tolerance and encouragement, this book could not have been written.

To Cork Millner, a well known Santa Barbara author, whose knowledgeable criticism continues to inspire me "to follow my dream."

To Commander Beverly Worden (U.S.N. Ret.), my brother's wife, whose spicy dissection and testing of the recipes has tempered and clarified their presentation.

And to Rae Hubbard, our friend and "the girl next door", who has, through countless patient hours, corrected the spelling and evolved the presentation of my ideas into a more precise and readable form.

And to the friends and family around my table who have urged me to "write it down."

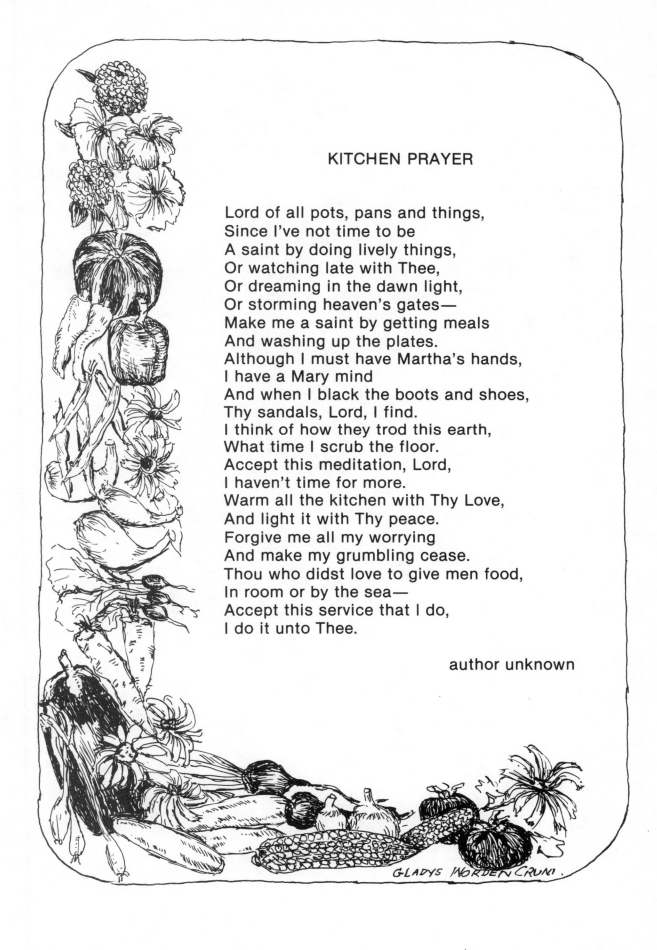

KITCHEN PRAYER

Lord of all pots, pans and things,
Since I've not time to be
A saint by doing lively things,
Or watching late with Thee,
Or dreaming in the dawn light,
Or storming heaven's gates—
Make me a saint by getting meals
And washing up the plates.
Although I must have Martha's hands,
I have a Mary mind
And when I black the boots and shoes,
Thy sandals, Lord, I find.
I think of how they trod this earth,
What time I scrub the floor.
Accept this meditation, Lord,
I haven't time for more.
Warm all the kitchen with Thy Love,
And light it with Thy peace.
Forgive me all my worrying
And make my grumbling cease.
Thou who didst love to give men food,
In room or by the sea—
Accept this service that I do,
I do it unto Thee.

author unknown

ABOUT THIS BOOK

This is about change - change in life styles and change in cooking styles, through three generations of collected recipes. The third generation having the completed advantage of being able to choose the most adaptable to its time and adding its own personal involvement.

San Francisco is the melting pot. The various nationalities there contribute to form the typical California characteristics found in these recipes. In this state today we spend more time out of doors. We respond quickly to innovation, to new products and new ideas. Some people even find us eccentric. We are informal. We set a bountiful table with less attention to detail and more to color, taste and pure enjoyment of the food we present.

This book does not attempt to follow haute cuisine, nor try to be trendy. It employs, rather, the simpler approach. One needs a stove, a refrigerator, utensils and ingredients; a sense of humor; patience; and an artistic appreciation of color and texture mixed with a tenacious determination to create quality, beauty, and tempting taste.

The reason we like cooking is that we like people. It is a form of communication. It pleases the tastes of others, as well as those of the cook. By organizing the thought process of food preparation through the senses, one profits by creative self expression, and shares the joys of accomplishment achieved in the kitchen.

So here they are: the selected recipes; the altered ones; the adapted ones and the created ones, — the final versions. These are presented in three sections: The German Heritage; The San Francisco Influence; and And Then There Is Me! — each with an introductory explanation. If you read this and it arouses your interest, then this is a good cook book and I will have fulfilled my desire to share recipes with you.

The world of food preparation is about the last frontier on earth. One can still explore new methods and combinations of ingredients, while utilizing and expanding the old.

Hopefully, you will find in these pages a curious and relaxed "fun exploration" in the art of good cooking.

CONTENTS

COOKING THROUGH THREE GENERATIONS, TITLE PAGE
DEDICATION
KITCHEN PRAYER
ABOUT THIS BOOK
CONTENTS   C-1   C-2
DEFINITIONS   D-1   D-2
IN MEASURING, REMEMBER   D-3

SECTION ONE, (DIVIDER) **THE GERMAN HERITAGE**
PREFACE   3
     MEATS   7 — 17
     VEGETABLES   18 — 24
     BREADS   25 — 29
     CAKES   30 — 34
     COOKIES   35
     SAUCES   36 — 39
     PRESERVES   40 — 42
     DESSERTS   43 — 46
     MISCELLANEOUS   48 — 51

SECTION TWO, (DIVIDER) **THE SAN FRANCISCO INFLUENCE**
PREFACE   55 — 56
     MEATS   59 — 66
     CHINESE SPECIALTIES   67 — 77
     ITALIAN SPECIALTIES   78 — 84
     FISH   85 — 90
     SALADS   91 — 98
     SALAD DRESSINGS   99 — 101
     CAKES   102 — 107
     COOKIES   108
     DESSERTS   109 — 113

CONTENTS (Continued)

SECTION THREE, (DIVIDER) **"AND THEN THERE IS ME!"**
PREFACE   117 — 119
     APPETIZERS   123 — 145
     MEATS   146 — 180
     POULTRY   181 — 185
     VEGETABLES   186 — 208
     FISH   209 — 225
     SOUTHWESTERN SPECIALTIES   226 — 253
     SALADS   254 — 269
     SALAD DRESSINGS   270 — 271
     SOUPS   272 — 275
     CAKES   276 — 282
     SAUCES   283 — 294
     BREADS   295 — 298
     SANDWICHES   299 — 303
     COOKIES   304 — 312
     DESSERTS   313 — 324
     PICKLES   325 — 329
     PRESERVES   330 — 337
     MISCELLANEOUS   338 — 341
ABOUT MENUS   343 — 347
INDEX   348 — 355
JUST IN THE NICK OF TIME   359 — 363

DEFINITIONS (PER AUTHOR)

A **ALTERNATE** — To do by turns.
APPROXIMATE — To come near to the correct amount.

B **BEAT** — To mix by stirring or striking repeatedly with a utensil.
BATCH — The amount of material needed in one operation.

C **CHOP** — To cut into small bits.
CREAM — To make into a creamy mixture.

D **DOLLOP** — A soft mass or blob.
DO IT YOURSELF — To create by oneself alone.

E **EFFORT** — A hard try; a diligent attempt.
EXPLAIN — A necessary procedure in the education of a cook.

F **FLUFFY** — Soft and light.
FOOD — Anything that nourishes and stimulates.

G **GOODIE** — Something considered very good to eat.
GLOM ON TO — To take and hold an idea.

H **HEAT** — Degree of hotness or warmth; a burning sensation produced by spices.
HEAP — To pile a plate full to overflowing with good food.

I **INGREDIENTS** — Any of the things of which a mixture is made.
INGENIOUS — What every cook strives to be; made or done in an original way.

J **JUICE** — The liquid part of food.
JUG — A container for liquid.

K **KITCHEN** — A room for the preparation of food. The heart of the home.
KEEP AT — to continue doing; to try again.

L **LABEL** — A mark to identify contents to avoid confusion.
LADLE — A longhandled cuplike spoon for transferring liquid from one place to another.

M **MEASURE** — The capacity of anything as determined by a standard.
MIX — To blend together in a single mass.

N **NEW** — Not yet familiar or accustomed.
NASTY — Offensive in taste or smell. (Hopefully never found in the kitchen.)

DEFINITIONS (continued)

O **OBTAIN** — To get possession of by some effort.

OLD — Familiar, or known from the past.

P **PINCH** — That which can be retained between the finger and the thumb.

PIECES — Parts or fragments broken or separated from the whole.

Q **QUALITY** — Any of the features that make something what it is.

QUINTESSENCE — The most perfect manifestation of a quality.

R **RELEVANT** — Related to the other matter in hand; implies close logical relationship with.

RECIPE — A list of materials and directions for preparing dishes or drink.

S **SMIDGE, SMIDGEON** — A small amount or bit.

SEASON — To make more tasty by adding salt or spices.

T **TASTER** — A person who indicates by the expression on his face whether or not a taste of food tastes good to him.

TENDER — Hopefully, a quality of the food one prepares; soft, delicate, easily chewed.

U **UNTIL** — To the point or degree that a preparation is done.

UTILIZE — To put to use, or make practical use of.

V **VARIETY** — Difference in color and texture in presentation of food. Absence of monotony.

VACUUM — A space with nothing at all in it.

W **WAX** — To become enthusiastic; to grow.

WELL — A depression on a platter or broiler for catching meat juices.

X **XANTHIPPE** — Socrate's quarrelsome and nagging wife, (what one can't be and enjoy working in the kitchen).

XEROX — A device for copying graphic or printed material.

Y **YEAST** — used as a leavening for bread.

YEAR — Three hundred sixty five days of which one does not have enough of, to explore the adventures of cooking good food.

Z **ZEST** — Something that gives flavor, piquancy and a keen enjoyment.

ZING — A lively zestful quality.

IN MEASURING, REMEMBER . . .

Bu.	Bushel — 48 lbs. or 4 pecks
C.	Cup — 16 tbs. — 8 oz. — 1 pt.
Ga.	Gallon
½	One half
¼	One quarter
Hr.	Hour
Lb.	Pound — 16 oz.
Min.	Minute
Oz.	Ounce — 2 tbs. of liquid
Pt.	Pint — 2 cups
Peck	8 qts.
Qt.	Quart — 4 cups — 2 pts.
Sq.	Square
Tbs.	Tablespoon — 4 tbs. = ¼ cup
Tsp.	Teaspoon — 3 tsp. = 1 tbs.

CUPS PER POUND

Butter, shortening, margarine — 2 cups = 1 lb. — 4 sticks
Eggs, large size, without shells — 2 cups = 1 lb.
Grated cheese — 4 cups = 1 lb.
Flour — 4 cups = 1 lb.
Shelled walnuts — 4 cups = 1 lb.
Sugar — 4 cups = 1 lb.

FACTS

Because ovens vary, the heating instructions in the following recipes are only guidelines.

As I am a "taste and tell" cook, the amounts of spices, etc., may also vary according to individual tastes.

Unless recipe explicitly explains differently, use a preheated oven.

When a recipe calls for butter, margarine may be used as an alternate unless indicated otherwise.

Section One

The German Heritage

THE GERMAN HERITAGE

Standing close to the large black iron stove, she looked even smaller than her five feet. Her stooped shoulders strained forward and her arm swung precariously near the stove top, as she reached towards the kettle.

An ever-present wheat colored crockery bowl, with a blue band skirting its middle, stood on top of the warming oven above, in which her "smierkase" (cottage cheese) was making.

Elise's salt and pepper hair was pulled neatly to the back, fastened by three or four bone hairpins. A white apron tied in back with a perky bow, billowed around her.

This was my groesmudder, (grandmother), or "Gapoo", as I had always called her. Born Elise Marie Waachhusen in Stuttgardt, Germany in the eighteen hundred sixties, she married John Stelling while in her teens. Together they came to America and to San Francisco around the Horn on a sailing ship. (I still have the iron ableskiever (pancake) pan she brought with her.)

In the early years in the City, John and Elise worked hard. They were frugal and they prospered. He opened a corner grocery store and she "did housework" for a wealthy San Francisco family. Elise bore six children. Four died before they reached the age of two. My mother, Dorathea, was the oldest of the six.

During the great earthquake and fire in San Francisco in nineteen hundred and six, Elise was the one who, in her neighborhood, had the presence of mind to turn on the water in the bathtub immediately. Before it was cut off, the water had nearly filled that tub. It was their only source of water for days. They moved the black iron stove out onto the street. That is where Elise cooked their meals.

After John died, she remained at home. She learned American ways, but clung to her hearty German Style of cooking. The kitchen was her private world, and oh! how she could cook! She wore a path on the linoleum floor of the huge high ceilinged kitchen from the stove to the large wooden table in the middle of the room, to the sink in the butler's pantry and across again to the back porch, where the ice box was. She baked, boiled and canned constantly. The San Francisco fog lurked outside the tall windows, or the golden sun streamed in. The smell of bread baking was synonymous with the place.

The canary sang in its cage.

The German words equivalent to the English recipe titles in Section One, "The German Heritage," may not be grammatically correct nor spelled correctly. They are as close to how I recall hearing them from my grandmother as memory will allow.

GLADYS WORDEN CRUTE

5

MEATS

BRAISED PICKLED BEEF POT ROAST — (SAUERBRATEN)
GERMAN STYLE BEEF BRISKET — (RINDFLEISCH MIT
    SAUERKRAUT)
MEAT PATTIES — (FRICKADELLEN)
HAM AND LAMB STEW — (VARESSEN) (WUDDLEMOUSSE)
OLD COUNTRY CABBAGE ROLLS — (KOHROLADEN)
PORK CHOPS AND APPLE CASSEROLE — (SCHEINEKOTELETTS
    MIT APFEL)
ROUND STEAK ROLLS — (ROULADEN)
SAUSAGE WITH SAUERKRAUT — (WURST MIT SAUERKRAUT)
SAUERKRAUT PORK POT ROAST — (SCHWEINEBRATEN MIT
    SAUERKRAUT)
VEAL CUTLETS — (KALBSS CHINTZEL)

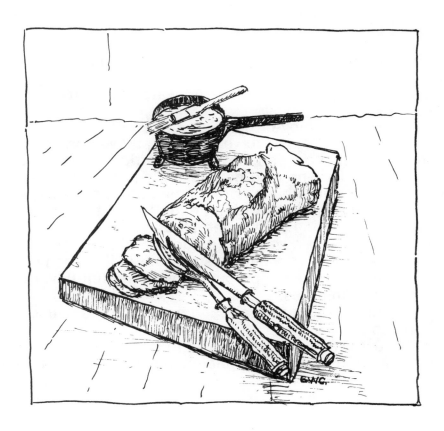

BRAISED PICKLED BEEF POT ROAST
(Sauerbraten)

4 lb. bottom sirloin butt
3 tbs. bacon drippings
2 large stalks celery
2 medium parsnips
4 medium carrots
2 medium yellow onions
6 tbs. red wine vinegar
1-¼ c. water
3 whole cloves
2 bay leaves
½ c. sour cream
salt and pepper to taste

- Peel and chop parsnips, carrots and onions coarsely.
- Chop celery.
- Mix vinegar, chopped vegetables and water. Bring to a boil in a medium pan.
- Cook 10 minutes. Remove from heat and cool.
- Add cloves and bay leaves to vegetables and vinegar. Pour over meat in a large shallow pan, cover, and refrigerate overnight. Baste occasionally. The next day, take meat from marinade and brown in a large pot in bacon drippings. Salt and pepper to taste.
- Strain marinade and dilute with an equal quantity of water. Add to browned roast along with vegetables.
- Simmer all until tender, basting frequently, about 1-½ to 2 hours.
- Stir in sour cream when meat is tender but still in the pot and simmer until it has been impregnated with the full flavor of the sauce, about 15 minutes.
- To serve, slice thin across grain and serve with its sauce over wide noodles.
- Serves 6 or 8. Delicious warmed over in its own juices.
- To freeze, separate meat from juices and vegetables, and freeze separately.

GERMAN STYLE BEEF BRISKET
(Rindfleisch Mit Sauerkraut)

4 lb. beef brisket
1 c. water
1 medium yellow onion
2 tsp. salt
½ tsp. pepper
1 tsp. caraway seeds
2 tbs. vinegar
2 bay leaves
2 tbs. brown sugar
1 large potato
1 l lb. 11 oz. can sauerkraut
2 tbs. bacon drippings

- Peel and quarter onion.
- Brown meat in bacon grease in a large pot roast pot.
- Add water, onion, salt, pepper, caraway seeds, vinegar and bay leaves.
- Cover and simmer 3 hours, until meat is very tender. (About 1 hr. per lb.)
- Peel and grate potato. Drain sauerkraut.
- Add brown sugar, potato and sauerkraut.
- Cover and cook 20 minutes over low heat.
- Makes 8 to 10 servings.

MEAT PATTIES
(Frickadellen)

2 c. tender cooked beef (left-over pot roast)
1 medium yellow onion
1 c. cooked mashed potatoes
½ tsp. salt
¼ tsp. pepper
3 tbs. butter or bacon drippings

- Peel and quarter onion.
- Run pieces of meat and onion quarters through a meat grinder, or chop very fine.
- Mix meat, onion and mashed potatoes well, adding salt and pepper to taste. Shape into 2 inch patties.
- Fry in butter or bacon drippings in an iron skillet about 5 minutes on each side, until crisp and brown on outside and soft and tender inside.
- These patties may be made ahead and frozen for future use. They are delicious served with Glad's Chile Sauce. (See index.)

I highly recommend using a heavy iron skillet for frying Frickadellen. It holds the heat evenly. After using, wash and dry thoroughly. Pour 1 tsp. vegetable oil in center of pan. Rub over inside surfaces with a paper towel, then wipe clean and dry. This keeps pan fresh and free from rust.

HAM AND LAMB STEW
(Varessen) (Wuddlemousse)

This is a German boiled dinner. Mutton was originally used with the ham. I find lamb, or even beef, a delicious substitute for the mutton. It has always been the custom to serve "Wuddlemousse," as my grandmother called it, on Christmas Eve. Along with biscuits to soak up the juice, it was a one dish meal. That meant fewer dishes to wash so that we could get on with our Christmas festivities as soon as the dishes were put away. We now have Wuddlemousse on Sunday nights or whenever a satisfying simple supper is called for, as well as on Christmas Eve.

The meal was served individually in a large soup bowl, each person ceremoniously cutting up the tender meat into small pieces and them mashing and mixing all the ingredients together in the dish before eating. Chopped sweet pickle relish and Worcestershire sauce were added over all. To this day the aroma of Wuddlemousse cooking on the stove reminds me that surely special delights must follow.

4 ham hocks or smoked ham pieces
4 lamb shanks, or 4 lamb chops, or 1 lb of either lamb or beef stew meat
4 carrots
4 turnips
4 or 5 medium potatoes
Chopped sweet pickle relish to taste
Worcestershire sauce to taste
Salt and pepper to taste

- Place ham, lamb shanks or lamb chops, or stew meat in a large stewing pot.
- If using beef, cut it into small 1 inch pieces.
- Cover with water and bring to a boil. Simmer until meat is tender, usually about 1-½ hours.
- Meanwhile peel and cut vegetables into 1 inch pieces. Hold all in a bowl of water until ready to use.
- About ½ hour before meat is done, drain vegetables and add them to the meat.
- Add a little more water if necessary. Cook about 15 minutes, adding salt and pepper to taste. Remove ham hocks and lamb shanks. Cut meat from bone. Discard bones and add meat pieces to vegetables in pot.
- Serve hot in large individual bowls. Pass the relish, worcestershire and more of the stewing juice. Mash together and enjoy.
- Serves 4 generously.

OLD COUNTRY CABBAGE ROLLS
(Kohroladen)

1 medium head cabbage
1-½ tsp. salt
1 tsp vinegar
½ c. instant rice
2 large stalks celery
2 tbs. butter
1 lb ground beef
1 egg
1 10-½ oz. can condensed tomato soup
2 tbs. red wine
1 tbs. dried parsley flakes
1 tbs. minced onion
1 6 oz. can tomato paste
4 slices bacon

- Mince onion.
- Dice celery.
- Cut core out of cabbage. In a large pot, place cabbage in water to cover.
- Add vinegar and salt. Bring to a boil, removing a few leaves at a time as they wilt. 18 leaves.
- Cook rice according to package directions.
- Saute celery in butter in a small frying pan for 5 minutes.
- Put meat in a large bowl and add egg, wine, parsley flakes, onion, celery and ½ can undiluted soup. Mix well.
- Place a spoonful of meat mixture in each leaf. Fold. Roll and secure with toothpicks.
- Arrange rolls close together in a large baking dish.
- Mix rest of soup, tomato paste and 1-½ soup cans of water and pour over cabbage rolls in baking pan.
- Cut bacon slices in half and place one on each cabbage roll, securing, if necessary, with a toothpick.
- Cover with lid or foil and bake in a preheated oven for 1 hour at 400 degrees. Lower to 350 degrees and bake ½ hour longer. Baste occasionally with the tomato sauce in the pan, adding a little water if necesary.
- Serves 6.

PORK CHOPS N' APPLE CASSEROLE
(Scheinekoteletts mit Apfel)

4 lean pork chops cut ½ inch thick
½ tsp. salt
1 tbs. vegetable shortening
4 tart Granny Smith apples
¼ c. raisins
1 small lemon
¼ c. molasses (light or dark)
¼ c. cold water
2 tbs. water

- Sprinkle salt in a large skillet. Fry pork chops in salt about 4 minutes each side until golden brown. (Add shortening if necessary to prevent sticking.)
- Peel, core and slice apples into 1/8 inch slices.
- Grate lemon rind to make 1 tsp.
- Mix apples slices, raisins and grated lemon rind and spread in a greased casserole.
- Combine molasses and water. Pour over apple mixture.
- Arrange browned pork chops over apples in casserole.
- Add 2 tbs. water to pan and scrape drippings over pork chops.
- Cover. Bake 1 hour at 350 degrees.
- Remove cover. Bake ½ hour longer until chops are tender.
- Serves 4.

ROUND STEAK ROLLS
(Rouladen)

This recipe was handed down by word of mouth. I also had the privilege of watching both my grandmother and mother prepare it. The round steak should be thin. You can usually get two rolls out of each thin slice of meat. Use the remaining pieces for stew. Always make at least two rolls per person or three for hearty eaters. They shrink a little while cooking. Rouladen may be made ahead and rewarmed in their own gravy.

4 slices round steak, cut thin
3 medium yellow onions
3 slices bacon
4 tbs. bacon drippings
2 c. water

Salt and pepper to taste
1 10-½ oz. can beef bouillon
3 tbs. flour
4 tbs. water

- Remove fat from round steak and cut meat in approximately 3 x 5 inch pieces. Lay them out on a board. Salt and pepper each piece.
- Peel and thinly slice onions. Cut bacon in thirds crosswise.
- Place ⅓ slice bacon across widest end of each piece of meat.
- Top each piece of bacon with 2 onion slices.
- Roll meat, starting with onion and bacon end. Tie meat roll top and bottom with cotton string.
- Heat bacon drippings in a large pan. (Cast iron pot roast pan is best.)
- Braise rolls, turning on all sides to brown. This takes about 10 minutes over medium heat.
- Set rolls aside as they are browned, doing all rolls in single layers.
- Replace all meat in pot. Pour water over and cover. Simmer about 1-½ hours or until tender. Add more water if necessary to prevent sticking.
- When tender, remove cover and turn heat to high to cook down most of the remaining liquid, being careful not to burn meat. (This browning is what gives the rolls their distinctive flavor.)
- Remove meat, cutting off cotton string-ties with scissors. Keep meat warm.
- Add rest of water to the pot, stirring to dislodge all bits and pieces from sides and bottom of pot.
- A cup of bouillon may be added at this point to supplement juices.
- Thicken gravy with a paste made from flour and water.
- When ready to serve, place rolls in gravy and heat. Pour gravy over rolls to serve.
- Serves 4.

SAUSAGE WITH SAUERKRAUT
(Wurst Mit Sauerkraut)

1-½ lb. Polish, smoked or other cooked sausage
1 medium yellow onion
1 medium tart apple
1 16 oz. can sauerkraut
1 tbs. brown sugar
1 tbs. dry sherry
½ tsp. caraway seed
1 10-½ oz. can beef broth
4 slices bacon

- Dice bacon.
- Peel and chop onion.
- Peel, core and dice apple.
- Drain sauerkraut well.
- Cut deep slashes in sausage at 1 inch intervals.
- In a large frying pan, cook bacon and onion until limp. Stir in sauerkraut, apple, sugar, sherry, caraway seed and ½ cup beef broth.
- Cook, stirring, for 2 minutes.
- Arrange sausage on top. Cover. Simmer 20 minutes, adding more broth if necessary.
- Serve with boiled potatoes.
- Serves 4.

SAUERKRAUT PORK POT ROAST
(Schweinebraten mit Sauerkraut)

1 4 lb. boned and rolled pork butt
1 bay leaf
1 1 lb. 11 oz. can sauerkraut
4 c. apple juice
8 small white onions
8 medium potatoes
8 medium carrots

- Drain sauerkraut.
- Peel and quarter potatoes.
- Peel onions.
- Pare and cut carrots in 2 inch pieces.
- Simmer pork in a large pot with bay leaf, sauerkraut and half the apple juice until well mixed and steamed about ¾ of an hour, stirring occasionally.
- Add vegetables, pour in remaining apple juice. Cover and simmer 1 hour longer, until meat is very tender and vegetables well done.
- Add a little water or apple juice if necessary.
- Serves 6 to 8.

VEAL CUTLETS
(Kalbss Chintzel)

½ c. flour
2 tbs. parmesan cheese
1 tsp. salt
½ tsp. pepper
2-½ lb. of veal steaks, cut thin
2 eggs
¼ c. fine bread crumbs
8 tbs. butter (¼ lb.)
2 tbs. lemon juice
3 sprigs fresh parsley

- Combine flour, salt, pepper and parmesan cheese.
- Pound veal steaks thin and cut into serving pieces.
- Beat eggs.
- Remove stems and chop flowerets of parsley to make about 2 tbs.
- Dip each piece of veal in the beaten egg and then in the bread crumbs, coating thoroughly.
- Melt half the butter in a large frying pan and place the veal pieces in it.
- Cook over medium heat until tender and well browned on both sides, about 5 minutes on each side.
- Remove meat and place on a platter to keep warm.
- Brown the rest of the butter in the frying pan.
- Add lemon juice and parsley and stir well. Pour over the meat and serve.
- Serves 4 to 6.

VEGETABLES

CARROTS, RHINELAND STYLE — (MOHREN RHEINLANDISCH)
GREEN BEANS WITH SWEET AND SOUR SAUCE AND BACON —
    (GRUENE BOHNEN MIT SPECK)
RED CABBAGE — (ROT KOHL)
POTATO PANCAKES — (BRATEN KARTOFFEL KUCHEN)
SAUERKRAUT
SAUERKRAUT WITH APPLES — (SAUERKRAUT MIT APFELEN)

CARROTS, RHINELAND STYLE
(Mohren Rheinlandisch)

8 medium carrots
1 tsp. sugar
3 Granny Smith apples
2 large yellow onions
2 tsp. bacon drippings
½ tsp. salt
¼ tsp. pepper
1 medium lemon

- Peel carrots. Slice lengthwise in ½ inch x 2 inch lengths.
- Peel and thinly slice onions.
- Squeeze lemon to make 2 tsp. juice.
- Peel, core and thinly slice apples. Hold in water until ready to use.
- Cook carrot strips in boiling water to cover, only until firm tender, about 5 minutes.
- Fry onions in bacon grease until golden brown. Add sugar, carrot strips and the water they were cooked in. Add apple slices and stir over medium heat until all ingredients are tender, about 5 minutes.
- Season with salt and pepper and just before serving, sprinkle with lemon juice.
- Serves 4.

GREEN BEANS WITH SWEET SOUR SAUCE AND BACON
(Gruene Bohnen mit Speck)

**1 lb. green string beans
6 bacon slices
1 medium yellow onion
1 tbs. vinegar
1 tbs. sugar
1 tbs. flour
Salt and pepper to taste**

- Peel and chop onion fine.
- Wash beans and break into short 1-½ inch lengths. Cook in salted boiling water for 10 minutes.
- Drain beans, saving about ¾ c. liquid and keep liquid warm.
- Dice bacon. Fry until crisp in a large pan. Remove bacon from the pan, saving about 2 tbs. of drippings in the pan.
- Fry onion in the bacon fat about 5 minutes until golden.
- Sprinkle flour over the onion. Let it cook for 2 or 3 minutes, stirring. Then add enough hot liquid from the beans to make a smooth sauce.
- Add salt and pepper to taste and the vinegar and sugar, stirring well.
- Add beans. Mix.
- Continue cooking over low heat until beans are tender, about 15 minutes, shaking the pan from time to time to prevent burning.
- Sprinkle bacon bits over top before serving.
- Serves 4.

Hint: When frying bacon, save any bacon drippings you don't use in a covered jar in the refrigerator. It's great in which to sear meats, and as a cooking and seasoning vehicle for vegetables.

RED CABBAGE
(Rot Kohl)

1 medium red cabbage
2 red firm apples
1 large yellow onion
¼ c. vinegar
2 tbs. bacon drippings
2 tbs. brown sugar
4 whole cloves
½ c. water
Salt and pepper to taste

- Remove coarse outer leaves and cut cabbage in half. Remove hard core.
- Finely shred cabbage.
- Peel, core and chop apples.
- Peel and coarsely chop onion.
- Melt bacon drippings in a thick bottomed saucepan.
- Add cabbage, apples, onion, sugar, cloves, vinegar and enough water to prevent burning. Cook over low heat.
- Cover, stirring frequently.
- Continue simmering until cabbage turns dark red, about 40 minutes, stirring occasionally and adding more water if needed.
- Salt and pepper to taste.
- Keeps well, covered, in refrigerator.
- Serves 6.

POTATO PANCAKES
(Braten Kartoffel Kuchen)

6 to 8 medium size potatoes
1 large yellow onion
2 eggs
2 rounded tbs. flour
Bacon drippings

- Peel potatoes. Shred fine.
- Peel onion. Shred fine.
- Place potatoes and onions in a large mixing bowl. Salt and pepper to taste.
- Beat eggs.
- Add eggs to vegetables. Mix well.
- Add flour. Beat again.
- Drop by tablespoonsful on a skillet greased with bacon drippings.
- Fry 5 minutes on each side until golden brown and crispy edged, and potatoes are done inside.
- Serve at once. Makes 8 to 10 pancakes.

SAUERKRAUT

Sauerkraut is probably the best of all known German vegetables, very prevalent in many German recipes.

Before the wide spread and convenient use of canned sauerkraut, it was made in large quantities at home in a clean wooden tub, rubbed inside with vinegar. The shredded cabbage, (my grandmother used fifty pounds of cabbage and two pounds of salt) was mixed with the salt and packed tightly into the tub. Then it was covered with a lid slightly smaller than the top of the tub and weighted down with a heavy object. This was left for about three weeks, being stirred once in a while with a clean wooden stick to let the gas escape. (I can remember the strong and pungent odor when this task was performed.)

When the cabbage was fermented, it was stored in a cool place in the basement. Instead of opening a can, we'd march down into the cool depths of the basement with a pan and a large slotted spoon, to scoop out the amount needed. Still, the sauerkraut recipe took hours to prepare, for it had to simmer first for a long time to be cooked and ready for use.

The recipes used in this book are old German ones, but we have altered them to use canned sauerkraut so easily available today.

SAUERKRAUT WITH APPLES
(Sauerkraut mit Apfelen)

1 16 oz. can sauerkraut
3 Granny Smith apples
1 medium yellow onion
2 tbs. bacon fat
¼ tsp. caraway seeds
1 tsp. sugar
3 tbs. flour
3 tbs. hot water
1 large baking potato
½ tsp. salt
¼ tsp. pepper

- Peel, core and slice apples into thin slices.
- Peel and thinly slice onion.
- Melt bacon fat in a large skillet.
- Drain sauerkraut and add to melted bacon grease. Fry for 2 minutes, stirring.
- Add hot water, apples, onion and sugar. Mix.
- Cook slowly about 30 minutes, until apples and onion are tender.
- Peel and coarsely grate potato. Add to sauerkraut.
- Mix flour with water. Add salt, pepper and caraway seed to sauerkraut.
- Stir in flour and water. Cook 10 minutes, stirring frequently.
- Delicious served with German sausage or frankfurters.
- Serves 4 to 6.

BREADS

ONE - TWO - THREE BREAD — (EINS - ZWEI - DREI BROT)
CINNAMON BUNS — (ZIMT BROTCHEN)
CRUST BOWLS — (KRUSTE SCHALE)

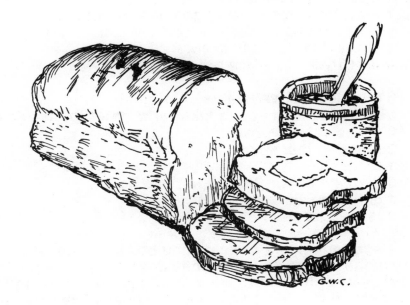

ONE-TWO-THREE BREAD
(Eins-Zwei-Drei Brot)

The miracle of bread: There they were: five bread pans in a row, bulging with high rounded loaves of homemade bread. Sunlight from the window blended into their warmth. What six hours earlier had been nothing but a large bowl and a few ingredients, now lay in a tempting buxom glow on the racks to cool.

Here is where the triumph and satisfaction of the cook actually seems to be shared by the beauty of the loaves themselves.

Be a magician! Try it! You'll know!

3 rounded tbs. vegetable shortening
½ c. milk plus enough lukewarm water to make a quart
2 cakes active yeast
2 rounded tbs. sugar
1 tbs. salt
5 lbs. and about 2 c. all-purpose flour
1 c. lukewarm water
1 tsp. sugar

- Plop the shortening in a large mixing bowl. (I use a stainless steel bowl 16 inches across and 6 inches deep.)
- Pour the quart of lukewarm water and milk over the shortening. Break apart the shortening as much as possible with a large mixing spoon.
- Dissolve the yeast cakes in 1 c. lukewarm water and 1 tsp. sugar. (The sugar makes the yeast activate faster.)
- Add sugar and salt to contents in pan. Mix.
- Add dissolved yeast and stir.
- Now add the flour gradually, not more than 2 to 3 cups at a time, stirring with a large spoon and scraping the sides and bottom of the bowl constantly to facilitate mixing.
- As you stir, add more flour until dough becomes sticky and too thick to handle with a spoon.
- Begin kneading with both floured hands, using a pull-from-sides and push-down-in-center motion, all the while scraping sides and bottom of pan and rotating it as you knead, to keep as clean of flour on the sides and bottom of the pan as possible.
- It will be sticky at first. Add more flour to your hands. As you continue this process, it will form a nice mass of dough and hopefully, with clean sides and bottom to the bowl. (Gapoo used to tell me that the sign of a good bread maker was the sight of a dough-free bowl.)

ONE-TWO-THREE BREAD (continued)
(Eins-Zwei-Drei Brot)

- When all the flour has been added, your kneading will have formed a good ball of bread dough. Round it out, turn it over and settle it comfortably in a slightly warm place, covered with a clean towel.
- Let rise to twice its size. This usually takes about 1-½ hours, depending upon surrounding temperature conditions. The warm sunlight is ideal. Room temperature about 72 to 74 degrees.
- Meanwhile, grease five 9 x 5 x 2-½ inch bread pans.
- When dough has risen, again pinch whole ball of dough and knead down. Cover with the kitchen towel again. Let rise until about twice its size, another 1-½ hours.
- After dough has risen the second time, pinch off 1/5 th portion. Knead that portion on a floured board with the same side-to-center-pinch-down motion. (You may hear little squeaks as air bubbles are squeezed out.) Proceed with other 4 separations and kneading and shaping into loaves one by one, placing each in its buttered bread pan. Poke each loaf along its top with the tines of a fork several times to make sure air bubbles are gone. (If there were holes in baked bread my grandmother used to say "That's where the baker chased his wife through!")
- Have the oven heated to 400 degrees.
- Bake all loaves at once on center oven rack for 1 hour. (It's a good idea to check the fit of your pans in the oven before heating.)
- Bake 20 minutes at 400 degrees, then at 350 degrees for another 40 minutes.
- Remove from oven and place on cooling wire racks for 10 minutes. Then remove loaves from pans and cool upright on racks.
- Makes 5 loaves.
- They can be frozen.

Too bad the aroma of that baked bread cannot be canned and used later!

CINNAMON BUNS
(Zimt Brotchen)

These are always made in conjunction with the making of One-Two-Three bread. Only after the second rising of the dough, instead of making five loaves, you make four, setting aside the fifth portion of dough for the buns. They will rise faster than the loaves, and will take less time to bake.

Pull apart to serve. Serve warm for breakfast or anytime. The amounts of butter, nuts and brown sugar used may vary according to your own preference. Delicious also, using pecans or almonds instead of walnuts.

> **One fifth portion of bread dough**
> **1-½ c. brown sugar**
> **½ c. melted butter**
> **1 c. chopped walnuts**
> **¾ cube butter**
> **4 tsp. cinnamon**

- Knead portion of bread dough, ready to rise for the third time, on a floured board.
- Roll out as hard as possible with a rolling pin after kneading, until it is spread to a ½ inch thin sheet. If the dough springs back too much, let it sit for 10 minutes, then roll out again.
- Spread with ¾ c. brown sugar, 2 tsp. cinnamon, ½ c. chopped walnuts and blobs of butter the size of large peas, cut off the cube of butter.
- Roll lengthwise, tucking in the contents spread on the sheet, as you roll.
- Slice completed roll of dough into 1-½ inch slices.
- Pour the melted butter over bottom of 9 x 12 x 2 inch baking pan.
- Sprinkle with rest of chopped nuts, 2 tsp. cinnamon and the rest of brown sugar.
- Arrange the slices in the pan, sides touching.
- Let rise ¾ hour or until about 2 inches high.
- Bake about 30 minutes, or until done, at 375 degrees. Turn out on a serving platter while hot, upside down, scraping any remaining candied sugar and nuts over the buns.
- Serve warm.
- Makes 8 to 12 buns.

CRUST BOWLS
(Cruste Schale)

Crust Bowls are made by using part of the bread dough as you are in the process of making bread. After the second rising and kneading (see index) take four lumps of twice kneaded dough, each about the size of a grapefruit. Knead them for the third time and place each in a greased small 6 x 3-½ inch bread pan, or on 4 small pie plates, if making round bowls.

When they have risen to about twice their size, bake along with the three other loaves of bread, at 400 degrees for 20 minutes and then at 350 degrees for 40 minutes, until crusty and golden. The small loaves will be quite crusty. Remove loaves at once to a wire rack to cool. When cool, they may be wrapped and frozen.

When ready to serve the Crust Bowls, cut about one quarter of the small loaf off the top. Scoop out the inner bread, leaving a 1 inch thick sided bowl. Warm the loaves. Butter them lightly in the inside. Fill with Sacramento Clam Chowder (see index), or a soup of your choice, preferably a thick soup. Or you may fill them with Campfire Chili (see index). Delicious, served with a green salad, and the talk of the town!

CAKES

COFFEE CAKE — (STRUSELKUCHEN)
FRUIT CAKE — (NAPFKUCHEN)
FRIED CAKES — (BACKPULVER KRAPEN)
OLD RELIABLE RAISIN CAKE — (RASINE KUCHEN)

COOKIES

NUTMEG SUGAR COOKIES — (MISKATNUB KLEINA STRUDEL)

COFFEE CAKE
(Struselkuchen)

This batter is enough for two coffee cakes in 9 x 9 inch pans, or one coffee cake and one fruit cake. (They may be frozen.)

1 cube butter (¼ lb.)
2 c. sugar
2 eggs
2 c. flour
2 tsp. baking powder
1 c. milk
1 tsp. almond flavoring
4 tbs. cinnamon
¾ c. coarsely chopped walnuts
½ cube butter

- Cream butter with 1-½ c. sugar.
- Add eggs and flavoring. Beat well.
- Add milk alternately with flour and baking powder. Beat.
- Spread ½ the batter in a 9 x 9 greased baking pan.
- Sprinkle the remaining sugar, (more, if desired) over the batter.
- Cover generously with cinnamon, walnuts and dots of butter cut off the cube.
- Bake in a 375 degree oven about 30 minutes, or until a cake tester thrust in center comes out clean.
- Let cool in pan.

Spread remaining batter in another greased 9 x 9 inch baking pan. Proceed with another coffee cake, or with a fruit cake (see index) as desired. Making one of each is a good combination, as one is for breakfast or lunch and the fruit cake is a dinner dessert.

FRUIT CAKE
(Napfkuchen)

This may be baked at the same time as the coffee cake (see index) using half the batter. However, it usually takes 5 to 10 minutes longer to bake, because of the moisture in the fruit.

1 16 oz. can apricot halves (canned plums or fresh fruit may be used)
¾ c. sugar
½ the batter from the coffee cake recipe

- Drain the fruit, if using canned fruit. Place the halves, rounded sides down on the batter spread in a 9 x 9 inch buttered pan, placing the halves close together. Cover the fruit with lots of sugar.
- Bake at 375 degrees about 45 minutes, or until cake tester thrust into cake comes out clean.
- Serve warm with whipped cream.
- This is a fine dessert and surprisingly easy to make. May be frozen.

FRIED CAKES
(Backpulver Krapen)

1 rounded tbs. butter
1 c. sugar
1 tsp. salt
2 eggs
½ c. milk
½ tsp. nutmeg
1 tsp. lemon flavoring
2 to 3 c. flour
2 to 3 c. vegetable shortening for deep frying
3 tsp. baking powder

- Blend butter and sugar in a large mixing bowl.
- Push to side of bowl. Beat eggs with a fork on other side of bowl.
- Add milk and flavorings. Mix all contents of bowl together well.
- Add flour, baking powder, salt and nutmeg. Beat.
- Add enough additional flour to make a soft dough that can be handled easily.
- Roll out on a floured board to between ½ and ¼ inches thick.
- Cut with a doughnut cutter. (Save the holes.)
- Put shortening in a deep iron pot. The melted grease should be about 3 inches deep.
- Heat to 360 degrees.
- Drop a few rings at a time into the hot shortening, turning each often until it is golden brown on both sides.
- Lift out with tongs onto paper towels to drain.

Today the doughnuts we enjoy are mostly "store made" and easily obtained. However, the aroma, sound and sight of these rings as each one floats golden and crisp to the top of the hot shortening, is plucked out with tongs at just the right moment and laid gently down on towels to cool, is a sensory experience and well worth the effort of preparation.

Grandmother saved the shortening for future fried cake making. It is a special treat to cook and eat the holes, too!

OLD RELIABLE RAISIN CAKE
(Rosine Kuchen)

It seems as if a pan of this cake, accompanied by a cake knife, was always available in grandmother's kitchen. Maybe that's why we all called it "Old Reliable." Part of the delight was that even the smaller children could come in from play and run to the cake pan, pick up the knife and cut out a square. It was best, of course, when still warm, but I can also recall having it for dessert with a warm custard sauce (see index) poured over it.

> 1-¼ c. brown sugar
> ½ c. shortening
> 2 eggs
> 1 c. sour milk
> 2 c. flour
> ½ tsp. salt
> 1 scant tsp. baking soda
> 1-½ tsp. cinnamon
> 1 tsp. nutmeg
> 1 c. raisins

- Cream shortening and sugar. Add eggs one at a time, stirring after each egg is added.
- Mix flour, salt, soda, cinnamon and nutmeg in a separate bowl.
- Add to creamed mixture alternately with sour milk. Beat.
- Add the raisins last. Mix well.
- Pour batter in a greased 9 x 9 x 2 inch square pan.
- Bake at 350 degrees about 45 minutes or until cake tester poked into the center comes out clean and a few small cracks show on surface of cake.
- Cool in the pan on a wire rack. (Then leave it within reach and see how long it lasts!)

Hint: If no sour milk is available, pour a cup of sweet milk and add 1 tsp. vinegar to it. Stir and let stand for ½ hour. Then use as sour milk. Do not use commercial sour cream when a recipe calls for sour milk, as it makes the cake too heavy and fine grained.

NUTMEG SUGAR COOKIES
(Miskatnub Kleina Strudel)

In the old high ceilinged kitchen, this ''little cake dough'' was rolled one half inch thick on the wooden work table. (Gapoo used a floured white kitchen towel on which to roll it.)

Cutting out the cookie circles, placing them on the cookie sheet with spatula and sprinkling sugar on each, was always a ceremony. The enjoyment was intensified when they were ready to be removed from the oven, warm and aromatic, to be slid gently onto another towel to cool. Then they were piled carefully so as not to spill the sugar and nut on top, into the cookie jar. (Sometimes Gapoo let a ''5 year old'' press half an almond in the center of each sugared circle before it went into the oven.)

> 1 c. sugar
> 2-½ c. flour
> 1 tsp. baking powder
> pinch of salt
> ½ c. shortening
> 1 egg
> ½ c. sour cream
> ½ tsp. baking soda
> ½ tsp. nutmeg, or to taste
> blanched almonds

- Beat egg. Add sour cream and soda. Mix sugar and shortening.
- Mix flour, baking powder, nutmeg and salt. Add alternately with egg and sour cream mixture to sugar mixture.
- Roll dough on a floured board to ¼ inch thickness. Do not make it too thick.
- Cut cookies with a cookie cuter. Place on a buttered cookie sheet with a spatula. Sprinkle each cookie with sugar. (Press a blanched almond half in center of each. Optional.)
- Bake 12 to 14 minutes at 375 degrees. Watch for edges to brown.
- Remove with a spatula to paper towels to cool.

These will keep well in a covered container. So good dunked in coffee, tea or milk.

SAUCES

CUSTARD SAUCE — (EIDOTTER SOBE)
HARD SAUCE — (SCHEIERIG SOBE)
SOFT SAUCE — (WEICH SOBE)

CUSTARD SAUCE
(Eidotter SoBe)

2 eggs
½ tsp. vanilla
2 c. milk
¼ c. sugar
¼ tsp. salt
1 tbs. cornstarch
1 tbs. water

- Separate eggs.
- Beat egg yolks. (Save whites for other uses.)
- Mix beaten yolks with ½ c. milk in a mixing bowl.
- Add sugar, salt and vanilla. Beat.
- Pour egg mixture in 1-½ c. of milk in a cooking pot, along with cornstarch mixed with water.
- Cook and stir, do not boil, about 5 minutes, or until of a custard consistency. Store in refrigerator. Serve at room temperature or warm over a piece of Old Reliable Raisin Cake (see index). Also delicious over Wine Jello (see index) for dessert.

Hint: If saving egg yolks, pour cold water over them and refrigerate covered for up to four days. No water is necessary for egg whites, only a lid.

HARD SAUCE
(Schierig SoBe)

1 c. powdered sugar
1 egg
Melted butter (In Grandmother's recipe it says, "the size of an egg.") Not having egg sizes of years ago, I guess about ½ cube of butter will do.
2 tbs. Bourbon whiskey or brandy

- Melt butter.
- Beat egg well and add slowly to the butter. Beat until frothy.
- Add powdered sugar gradually, beating after each addition.
- Add liquor. Mix well.
- Sauce should be of soft "frosting" consistency.
- Serve at room temperature.

This was always served on mince pie or with plum or carrot pudding at Christmas time. It's a tasty touch any time of the year, with a slice of Applesauce Cake (see index), or Golden Pound Cake (see index).

SOFT SAUCE
(Weich SoBe)

This sauce may be served over Rote Gruize, (see index), a red tapioca pudding, to add a tangy flavor. The ''vanilla cream'' mentioned in the Red Tapioca Pudding recipe is for those who do not care for the liquor flavoring or for kids sitting at the family table at holiday time, to pour over mince pie or plum pudding.

½ c. sugar
2 tbs. flour
1 tbs. butter
2 c. boiling water
1 tbs. brandy, or to taste

- Combine the sugar and flour and mix well in the top of a double boiler.
- Add the boiling water, stirring constantly to prevent lumping.
- Cook in the double boiler until mixture thickens to a thin creamy consistency. Stir often.
- Add butter and stir until melted. Add brandy.
- Serve warm in a pouring pitcher.
- Makes about 2 cups.

PRESERVES

APPLE BUTTER — (APFEL BUTTER)
LEMON BUTTER — (CITRONE BUTTER)

APPLE BUTTER
(Apfel Butter)

5 lb. Granny Smith apples
1 qt. apple cider
4-½ c. sugar
2 tsp. cinnamon
½ tsp. allspice
¾ tsp. cloves
¼ tsp. salt

- Wash and cut apples into small pieces. Do not peel or core.
- Add cider and bring to a boil in a large kettle.
- Simmer until apples are soft, stirring frequently, about 30 minutes.
- Press apples and juice through a sieve to separate pulp from seeds and skins.
- Add sugar, salt, cinnamon, cloves and allspice to pulp and juice.
- Cook in a large kettle until it thickens, approximately 45 to 60 minutes.
- Stir often.
- Pour into hot sterilized jars to ½ inch of the top.
- Seal while hot with melted paraffin.
- This is perfect on One-Two-Three bread. (See index.)

LEMON BUTTER
(Citrone Butter)

2 c. sugar
½ c. butter
3 eggs
½ c. water
3 large lemons

- Beat eggs.
- Cream butter and sugar thoroughly.
- Add beaten eggs and mix well.
- Grate rind of lemons. Add water, rind and juice of lemons to creamed mixture.
- Cook in top of double boiler until thick, about 15 minutes.
- Use as a filling for tarts, or as a spread on bread.
- Keeps well in the refrigerator.
- Makes about 2 cups.

DESSERTS

APRICOT BREAD PUDDING — (APRITOSE BROT PUDDING)
OLD FASHIONED RICE PUDDING — (ALTMODISCH REIS PUDDING)
RED TAPIOCA PUDDING — (ROTE CRUIZE)

APRICOT BREAD PUDDING
(Apritose Brot Pudding)

6 to 8 slices fresh white bread
2 c. milk
½ c. sugar
2 eggs
¼ tsp. salt
1 tsp. cinnamon
¼ lb. dried apricots

- Cut apricots with a scissors into small pieces about the size of raisins, to make ¼ cup.
- Cut off any heavy crusts of bread. Tear bread slices into approximately 1 inch pieces.
- Preheat oven to 350 degrees.
- Lightly beat eggs.
- Scald milk.
- Mix eggs, sugar, salt, apricots, cinnamon, milk and bread pieces.
- Pour mixture into a 2 qt. glass baking dish. Place in a pan of water 1 inch deep.
- Bake 1 hour until a knife inserted in center comes out clean.
- Makes 6 servings.
- Serve with cream.
- This pudding may also be made with raisins instead of dried apricots.

OLD FASHIONED RICE PUDDING
(Altmodisch Reis Pudding)

1 c. cooked rice
2 c. milk
¾ c. sugar
¼ tsp. salt
3 eggs
1 tsp. vanilla
½ c. raisins
nutmeg

- Beat eggs.
- Mix rice, milk, eggs, sugar, salt and vanilla.
- Add raisins and nutmeg last. Mix well.
- Pour into a 2 qt. glass baking dish. Place dish in a pan of water 1 inch deep to prevent pudding from sticking to dish.
- Bake uncovered at 400 degrees for 1 hour, until a knife inserted in center comes out clean.
- Serve at room temperature with cream, or Soft Sauce. (See index.)

RED TAPIOCA PUDDING
(Rote Cruize)

This is a "modern version" of the original tapioca pudding. I do not have the original recipe. I don't believe Elise Marie Wachhusen had one either. However, this looks and tastes like the original. We used to have this with some cream sweetened with a little sugar and flavored with vanilla, to pour over the top, "Vanille Kram", as grandmother used to say. I suspect it was a sweet substitute for the "Soft Sauce" served to "grownups." (See index.)

1 pkg. vanilla tapioca pudding
¾ c. water
½ c. Burgundy wine
1 pkg. frozen red raspberries
Fresh mint leaves, (optional)

- Combine the tapioca pudding, water and wine in a saucepan.
- Add frozen raspberries. Cook and stir until mixture comes to a full boil and is slightly thickened. It will continue to thicken as it cools. Stir once or twice, just to mix.
- Pour into individual serving glasses and chill at least 3 hours, or overnight.
- To keep the top soft, place a piece of plastic wrap on the top of each serving, while still warm.
- Serve with Soft Sauce. (See index.) Garnish with mint leaves.
- Serves 4.

THE CANARY SANG IN HIS CAGE —   GLADYS CRUM '86

47

MISCELLANEOUS

COTTAGE CHEESE — (SMIERKASE)
COUNTRY FRIED APPLES — (BRATPFANNE APFELEN)
DANISH DOUGHNUTS — (AEBLESKIVERS)

COTTAGE CHEESE
(Smierkase)

This is the original recipe — the way my grandmother made her cheese by keeping it in a large crockery pot on top of the warming oven of the big stove. It took three or four days to form and there always seemed to be a "working" crock above her as she cooked.

The bag of cheese was slung over a strainer perched in the crock, in the cheesecloth bag, where it would remain, dripping, until "the whey was all" and the cheese was ready to use. Sometimes this would take a week or more, depending upon the temperature and milk quality and age. When ready, the cheese was smooth, creamy and mild. It was used in cooking, with fruit to accompany meat and potato dinners, and mostly just to spread on bread or cookies anytime.

I can still taste smierkase spread on homemade bread with lots of salt and pepper on it. It was of a finer, creamier texture than the cottage cheese we buy today, although I must admit it is much easier to obtain it in the carton, than make it Gapoo's way.

1 qt. sour milk
1 qt. warm water

- Pour 1 qt. sour milk heated to lukewarm into a cheese cloth bag. Pour warm water over this after hanging the bag in top of a deep container.
- After the warm water has dripped through, repeat twice. Tie bag and let drip into the crock until the "whey is all." That is, when the liquid has completely drained out and the smooth curds remain in the cheesecloth bag.
- Serve with either sweet or sour cream to taste, and salt and pepper.
- Makes about a cup of smierkase.

In the days when children broadened their horizons by listening to fairy tales and nursery rhymes, this recipe recalls to my mind:

"Little Miss Muffet
Sat on a tuffet
Eating of curds and whey,
Along came a spider
Who sat down beside her
And frightened Miss Muffet away!"

COUNTRY FRIED APPLES
(Bratpfanne Apfelen)

6 firm tart apples
½ c. bacon drippings
⅓ c. sugar
¼ tsp. salt

- Peel, quarter and core apples. Cut into eighths. Or peel, core with an apple corer, and slice into ¼ inch rings. If cooking eighth slices, more than a single layer may be cooked at once. The apple rings are prettier, and hold their shape, if cooked in a single layer.
- Place slices in heated bacon drippings in a frying pan.
- Cover and cook briskly until apples are soft and there is little juice left in the pan.
- Stir gently, or turn rings, and cook briskly until liquid evaporates and apples are quite brown.
- These are delightful served with aebleskivers, (see index), pork sausages, bacon or ham for that special breakfast.
- Serves 6.

DANISH DOUGHNUTS
(Aebleskivers)

The Aebleskiver pan that my grandmother brought from Germany is very heavy and at least fourteen inches in diameter. It is made of cast iron and has seven hemispherical depressions measuring three inches in diameter and about one inch deep in its surface. They are coated with white porcelain. The long heavy handle becomes very hot when in use. An iron pan is best, for it distributes the heat evenly over the whole pan.

Today Aebleskiver pans are readily purchased in specialty cooking utensil stores. I have seen an electric one but have never tried it. This is the original recipe.

4 eggs	**¼ c. melted butter**
1 tbs. sugar	**½ c. milk**
2 c. flour	**½ c. shortening**
½ tsp. salt	**½ c. powdered sugar**
1 tsp. baking powder	

- Separate eggs. Beat egg yolks until light. Add sugar. Beat.
- Add dry ingredients to egg and sugar mixture alternately with melted butter and enough milk to make a heavy batter.
- Beat egg whites until stiff. Fold into the batter.
- Over medium heat spoon ½ tsp. shortening into each depression of the pan.
- Fill each ⅔ full with batter and cook slowly until bottom is lightly browned and edges begin to crisp, about 4 minutes, depending upon heat of pan.
- With an ice pick, a metal knitting needle or a fork, turn the balls over and brown the other side. Add a little more shortening if necessary. Be sure the center is done.
- Remove balls to an oven proof plate and dust with powdered sugar.
- Keep warm in oven until all are made, (if you can!).
- Delicious served for breakfast with pork sausages, applesauce or jam, or with slow fried smoked pork chops and Country Fried Apples (see index), for brunch or supper.

German pork sausages were cooked in a special fashion, by arranging them in a single layer in a shallow skillet, covered with cold water. Brought to a full boil, they were then drained at once, covered with 1 cup apple juice and simmered until the apple juice had cooked down and the sausages were browned and glazed. Simply delicious.

Section Two

The San Francisco Influence

THE SAN FRANCISCO INFLUENCE

"Why do you put empty plates on the table?" I asked my mother. "Seems silly."

"Because Emily Post says that a place setting at the table should never be empty. As the food is put before the guest, the place plate is taken away," she replied, as she glanced over the bounteous table set for eight. "Umm," I mumbled, not convinced that it wasn't silly and a lot of unnecessary work, at that. But if Emily Post's Book of Etiquette detailed that that was the way it was done, it was done that way and no other. That book was mother's guide to the correct social graces. She arranged the plates meticulously, while I put the silver services in proper order on each side, being careful that their bottom tips lined up exactly with the bottom edge of the plate. And so it was.

Dorathea Margaretha Stelling was born in San Franciso in eighteen hundred and eighty seven, destined to grow and change, along with the boisterous City. My grandmother was determind that her daughter should have the advantages that she didn't have. She strove through the frugal work-filled days to foster Dora's education. After high school, Dora went to the Mark Hopkins School of the Arts on the site where the Mark Hopkins Hotel now stands. Then Dorathea completed business college on Market Street.

Two weeks after the San Francisco earthquake and fire in nineteen hundred and six, on Dora's nineteenth birthday, her friend William Worden somehow managed, by scouting far afield, to find a fresh bottle of milk, which he brought to her. In that ravaged city, that was the most thoughtful and astonishing present she could have received.

A year later Dora married Will, a match not at first to her mother's liking, because Will lacked the finances when they were first married that she felt were necessary for the completion of Dora's "becoming a lady". However, Will prospered. He became involved in San Francisco politics. He was Director of the Board of Public Works in San Francisco for a number of years, and was active in the planning of the Bay Bridge. On opening day, he was among the group of dignitaries who attended the initial ceremonies.

Dora had no time for the joys of a creative kitchen. Her social obligations were numerous. She was in fragile health and lived under the constant stress of "keeping up with the whirl." Gentle and quiet by nature, she really preferred the simpler life.

THE SAN FRANCISCO INFLUENCE (continued)

Dora's cooking involved either planning for dinner parties at home, where she had "help" in the kitchen, or a reversion on other days to the hearty simple "meat and potato" style of her heritage. However, the short cuts, the easier methods of using canned soups and vegetables and instant foods gradually became more prevalent.

The life style of the nineteen twenties and thirties encouraged less emphasis on tedious methods of cooking and more use of newer products. That did not mean that either one or the other was "better", only that as the years progressed, newer adaptations often supplemented the old time consuming ways with which she had grown familiar.

She was a beautiful woman. I can remember standing by her dressing table watching her brush her waist length hair in long strokes, her head cocked to one side and then the other, the brush going up and down in sweet rhythm. She piled it high on her head in silken chestnut rolls in the style of the day. Her waist was slim and she held her head high. Dorathea bore two children and was a loving, though overburdened wife and mother. She was torn between the easy comfortable ways of her German background and the pressure of living up to the political and social obligations, basically foreign to her nature, that Will's status in San Francisco entailed. She emanated the graces of living and gave to those around her a sweet and gentle path to follow.

GLADYS WORDEN CRUM.

MEATS

BEEF STROGANOFF
JOE'S SPECIAL
OLD FASHIONED MEAT LOAF
SHORT RIBS OF BEEF
SWEET AND SOUR MEAT BALLS
YUM YUM BALLS
PARMESAN STEAK

GLADYS WORDEN CRUM '87

BEEF STROGANOFF

2-½ lb. slice of round steak cut ½ inch thick
¼ c. cooking oil
1 tsp. salt
¼ tsp. pepper
¼ c. red wine
1 c. small whole white onions
2 c. fresh mushrooms
¼ c. tomato paste
3 tbs. flour
1 10-½ oz. can consomme
1 bay leaf
1 clove garlic
½ c. sour cream

- Cut meat in serving size pieces.
- Brown in oil in a large frying pan.
- Transfer to a 3 qt. casserole.
- Sprinkle with salt, pepper and wine.
- Peel onions. Mince garlic.
- Wash, pat dry and slice mushrooms.
- Saute onions and garlic in frying pan drippings until golden.
- Add mushrooms to onions and cook 5 minutes.
- Mix tomato paste, flour and undiluted consomme.
- Add to vegetables in pan, along with bay leaf. Stir and simmer 5 minutes.
- Mix and pour over meat in casserole. Cover.
- Bake in a 350 degree oven, covered, for 1 hr.
- When meat is tender, remove casserole from oven and stir in sour cream.
- Serve hot over buttered noodles.
- Serves 8.

JOE'S SPECIAL

Joe's was located on Broadway at the corner of Columbus in the Italian Quarter of San Franciso. It was a small distinctive restaurant with a San Francisco "counter" atmosphere. Noisy and personable, the place abounded with good camaraderie and great food at any time of the day or night.

We first enjoyed their "Special" after an evening of dancing when I was in college in Berkeley. It became a standby over the years for almost anytime, and we now have "Joe's Special" often for breakfast, lunch or dinner.

But it tasted best at the counter, at Joe's.

1 10 oz. pkg. frozen chopped spinach
1 tbs. olive oil
1 tbs. butter
1 lb. ground beef
1 medium yellow onion
4 eggs
½ tsp. basil
¼ tsp. marjoram
¼ tsp. oregano
1 tsp. salt
¼ tsp. pepper

- Thaw spinach and drain well, squeezing out all excess water.
- Cook meat in olive oil until crumbly.
- Peel and chop onion. Add to meat and cook until soft, about 5 minutes.
- Add basil, marjoram, oregano, salt and pepper.
- Add spinach. Mix well.
- Cook until liquid in spinach is evaporated, stirring frequently.
- Beat eggs. Pour over spinach and meat. Cook until eggs are set, stirring.
- Serve immediately, with toasted french bread.
- Serves 2 generously.

OLD FASHIONED MEAT LOAF

1 lb. ground beef	3 slices bacon
1 egg	2 medium yellow onions
5 slices white bread	1 small yellow onion
½ tsp. salt	paprika
¼ tsp. pepper	¼ c. water

- Place ground beef in a large mixing bowl.
- Run bread slices under hot water until they are damp. Then immediately squeeze out as much water as possible. Crumble into meat.
- Peel and finely chop small onion to make 1 tbs.
- Peel and quarter medium onions.
- Salt and pepper the meat to taste, mixing with a fork.
- Add egg. Mix and knead with hands. Shape into a loaf when well mixed.
- Place in a baking pan large enough to hold loaf and the 8 onion quarters around the loaf.
- Cut bacon slices in half and lay halves crosswise across loaf, securing each end of each piece with a verticle toothpick.
- Sprinkle loaf lightly with paprika.
- Pour ½ c. water over onion quarters.
- Bake in a 350 degree oven for half to ¾ of an hour until bacon and onion are crisp and meat is cooked through. Add a bit more water if pan becomes too dry. Break up onions slightly after baking about 15 minutes.
- Drain grease from pan.
- Serve slices of meat with pieces of onion and meat juices. If you wish, thicken the juices with a little flour and water to make a thicker gravy.

For another meal — take ½ inch left over slices, fry gently in butter and serve with a gravy over each slice made with ½ c. milk and 1 11-oz. can cream of mushroom soup. Add 2 tsp. horseradish, or to taste.

Meat loaf is also delicious warmed over in some of Glad's Chili Sauce (see index). Be sure the slices are thick enough so that they will not break up when frying.

SHORT RIBS OF BEEF

3 lbs. beef short ribs
3 tbs. bacon drippings
1 tsp. salt
½ tsp. pepper
2 medium yellow onions
½ tsp. dry mustard
2 tbs. lemon juice
2 bay leaves
1-½ c. water
¼ c. brown sugar
1 10 oz. package frozen lima beans
3 medium carrots

- Brown short ribs in a large deep skillet or dutch oven in bacon grease.
- Peel and slice onions in ¼ inch slices.
- Salt and pepper to taste.
- Add onions, mustard, bay leaves, lemon juice and water to pot. Sprinkle brown sugar over ribs.
- Cook on low heat, covered, about 2 hours, turning meat occasionally and adding more water if necessary to prevent meat from sticking.
- Peel and cut carrots into 3 inch long ¼ inch wide strips.
- Add carrots and lima beans when meat is tender. Cook on moderate heat until vegetables are tender, about 15 minutes.
- Serve ribs with vegetables and juices.
- Serves 4.

SWEET AND SOUR MEAT BALLS

1 lb. ground beef
2 tbs. cooking oil
1 medium yellow onion
1 egg
6 to 8 parsley sprigs
⅓ c. water
¼ c. stale bread crumbs
1 tsp. salt
¼ tsp. pepper
¼ tsp. each, thyme and oregano
½ c. catsup or Glad's Chili Sauce (see index)
¼ c. honey
1 tsp. Dijon mustard

- Peel and mince onion to make about 3 tbs.
- Wash parsley, discard stems and mince flowerets to make about ½ cup.
- Mix meat, onion, parsley, thyme, oregano, salt and pepper.
- Add bread crumbs and slightly beaten egg. Mix well.
- Make into 1 inch balls. Roll balls in flour.
- Brown on all sides in cooking oil in a large skillet.
- Mix catsup, or chili sauce, mustard and honey and pour over the browned meat balls.
- Cover and simmer, turning occasionally, about 20 minutes until cooked through.
- These may either be served as an hors d'oeuvre on toothpicks, or with rice as a light meal.
- Makes 12 to 16 meat balls.

YUM-YUM BALLS

1 lb. ground beef
½ lb. ground pork
1 medium yellow onion
½ c. uncooked rice
½ c. bread crumbs
1 egg
½ tsp. salt
Dash of pepper
1 10-½ oz. can tomato soup
1 soup can of water

- Peel and mince onion.
- Mix meats, rice, bread crumbs, egg, onion, salt and pepper.
- Shape into 2 inch balls and place in a single layer in a greased casserole.
- Mix soup and water and pour over meat balls.
- Bake at 375 degrees for 1 hour or until rice is done. Turn occasionally and add a bit more water if necessary.
- A half cup of Glad's Chili Sauce (see index) added to the soup mix greatly enchances the flavor.

PARMESAN STEAKS

4 beef cubed steaks, single serving size
1 egg
1 tbs. water
¼ tsp. pepper
¼ tsp. salt
¼ c. fine bread crumbs
¼ c. grated Parmesan cheese
4 tbs. cooking oil
1 c. Glad's Chili Sauce (see index)

- Beat together egg, water, salt and pepper in a shallow dish large enough to hold 1 steak.
- Combine crumbs and ½ the cheese in a shallow bowl or dish.
- Dip cubed steaks in egg mixture, then in crumbs to coat well.
- Heat oil in a large skillet and brown steaks for about 3 minutes on each side until brown. Remove and drain on paper towels.
- Arrange the 4 steaks flat in a shallow baking dish. Pour Chili Sauce over them and sprinkle with remaining cheese.
- Bake uncovered in a 325 degree oven, basting once or twice, for 20 minutes.
- Serves 4.

To achieve an Italian flavor, use pizza sauce in place of the chili sauce. Serve with toasted Italian bread, a crisp salad and Chianti wine.

CHINESE SPECIALTIES

BARBECUED CHINESE PORK KABOBS
CHICKEN WINGS ORIENTAL
CHINESE BARBECUED DRUMSTICKS
CHINESE CRAB CAKES
CHINESE RICE
MANDARIN PORK
ORIENTAL BEEF LIVER
SWEET AND SOUR SAUCE

BARBECUED CHINESE PORK KABOBS

1 lb. lean pork
1 16 oz. can pineapple chunks
1 large green pepper
¼ c. soy sauce
2 tbs. olive oil
2 cloves garlic
¼ tsp. sugar
1 tsp. chili powder
¼ tsp. ground cloves
¼ tsp. ground cinnamon

- Cut pork into 2 inch cubes.
- Place in a shallow pan.
- Peel and mince garlic.
- Mix soy sauce, olive oil, garlic, sugar, chili powder, cloves and cinnamon.
- Pour marinade over pork. Marinate for several hours, turning occsionally to cover all sides of the meat cubes.
- Wash green pepper, removing membranes and seeds and cut into bite size pieces.
- Parboil for 2 minutes only until crisp tender. Drain.
- Drain pineapple chunks.
- Place 1 cube of pork, a piece of green pepper and a chunk of pineapple alternately on a skewer. Repeat twice.
- Barbecue about 5 inches above coals for about 10 minutes, turning to cook all sides and until meat is done to your liking and crisp on the edges.
- Push off of skewer and onto a plate to serve.
- Serves 4.
- Serve with Chinese rice. (See index.)

GRANT AVE. STORE, CHINATOWN.   GLADYS CRUM '86

CHICKEN WINGS, ORIENTAL

24 drummettes (major half of wings)
½ c. soy sauce
½ c. dark brown sugar
⅓ c. sherry wine
2 cloves garlic
1 tsp. ginger powder
1 tsp. sesame oil
½ tsp. hot pepper sauce
¼ tsp. cinnamon

- If you purchase whole chicken wings, cut off the smaller half of each wing. Save to make chicken broth. The larger half can be purchased at the supermarket under the name "Drummettes."
- Arrange chicken parts in a single layer in a baking dish.
- Peel and mince garlic.
- Combine soy sauce, brown sugar, sherry, garlic, ginger, sesame oil, hot pepper sauce and cinnamon and spoon over the chicken wing parts.
- Marinate, covered loosely and chilled 2 to 8 hours. Turn once or twice to cover all sides with marinade.
- Bake at 400 degrees, basting and turning several times for about 40 minutes, until tender and well glazed.
- These make delicious hors d'oeuvres, served either at room temperature or warm.

Serve on small cocktail plates, with napkins!

CHINESE BARBECUED DRUMSTICKS

8 chicken legs
½ c. soy sauce
½ c. orange juice
2 tbs. sherry wine
1 clove garlic
1 tsp. powdered ginger
3 tbs. brown sugar

- Parboil chicken legs in water for 10 minutes. Drain and cool.
- Cut skin in large diamond pattern with knife.
- Peel and mince garlic.
- Mix soy sauce, orange juice, sherry wine, garlic, ginger and brown sugar.
- Pour over chicken pieces. Marinate for several hours or overnight in the refrigerator, covered, turning 2 or 3 times to coat thoroughly with marinade.
- Bake at 375 degrees in a shallow baking dish, in their marinade, basting often until tender, about 25 to 30 minutes. Sauce will become thick and sticky.
- Or broil about 5 inches from heat, basting and turning several times until tender and brown, 6 to 8 minutes or until chicken meat is tender.

CHINESE CRAB CAKES

½ tsp. hot pepper sauce
6 eggs
1 c. fresh bean sprouts
1 7 oz. can crab meat, or ½ c. fresh crab meat
4 green onions
1 tsp. cooking oil

- Slice green onions thin crosswise, including about 2 inches of their stalks.
- Beat eggs. Add pepper sauce. Mix well.
- Stir bean sprouts, crab and onions into beaten eggs.
- Heat oil in skillet. Spoon a tablespoon full of the mixture into the pan to form a cake, making a single layer of cakes only.
- Cook until lightly browned, about 3 minutes on each side. Remove from skillet to a warm plate. Keep warm until all cakes are made. Add a little more oil if needed.
- Stack the crab cakes, 2 to a serving. Serve with Sweet-Sour Sauce (see index).
- Serves 4, in combination with chinese rice (see index) and Chinese vegetables cooked "al dente."

CHINESE RICE

2 c. cooked rice
2 small yellow onions
2 tsp. soy sauce
2 tbs. butter
½ tsp. salt

- Peel and finely chop onions. Saute 2 minutes in butter until golden.
- Add salt.
- Add rice and soy sauce. Mix.
- Serves 4.

Although plain rice is always correct for oriental dishes, the extra touch in this easy recipe adds to any Chinese cuisine.

MANDARIN PORK

2 lbs. pork loin
½ c. flour
½ c. oil
4 medium green peppers
1 large yellow onion
½ c. soy sauce
½ c. sherry wine
2 tbs. vinegar
1 tbs. sugar
3 medium carrots
1 15 oz. can pineapple chunks

- Cut meat into ½ inch cubes.
- Peel and cut carrots into ½ inch wide slices crosswise. Cook until just tender, about 10 minutes. Drain and set aside.
- Flour meat cubes. Saute in hot oil in a large skillet.
- Remove meat from pan.
- Wash, remove membranes and seed from green peppers. Cut into 1 inch pieces.
- Peel and cut onions into ½ inch thick slices.
- Add green pepper and onions to skillet and saute 2 minutes.
- Return meat to skillet and cook until vegetables are tender and meat is done, about 30 minutes, stirring occasionally.
- Drain pineapple. Save juice.
- Combine juice, soy sauce, sherry, vinegar and sugar.
- Stir and add to pork.
- Simmer 5 minutes.
- Add pineapple chunks and cooked carrots. Cook 2 minutes more, stirring well until meat is hot.
- Serve with Chinese rice (see index).
- Serves 4 to 6.

ORIENTAL BEEF LIVER

Salt and pepper to taste
3 tsp. olive oil
1 large yellow onion
2 cloves garlic
8 or 10 fresh mushrooms (½ lb.)
½ lb. beef liver
1 pkg. frozen Chinese pea pods
2 tbs. soy sauce
2 tsp. cornstarch
4 tbs. white wine

- Peel and cut onions into ¼ inch wedges.
- Mince garlic.
- Wash, pat dry and slice mushrooms.
- Wash, drain in a colander and cut membranes from liver. Cut into ½ inch strips.
- In a small bowl, blend soy sauce, cornstarch and wine.
- Heat oil in a large skillet. Add onion wedges, garlic and sliced mushrooms.
- Saute over high heat until tender, stirring, about 3 minutes.
- Stir in strips of liver and 1 cup pea pods. (If using frozen pods defrost them in a colander by running cold water over them before using.)
- Stir the soy sauce mixture into vegetable and beef in skillet.
- Cook until glazed an shiny, about 5 minutes, stirring constantly.
- Serves 2 generously.
- Serve with Chinese rice (see index).

SWEET AND SOUR SAUCE

2 tsp. sugar
1-½ tsp. cornstarch
2 tsp. vinegar
1 tbs. soy sauce
¼ tsp. hot pepper sauce
¾ c. water

- Combine sugar, cornstarch, vinegar, soy sauce, pepper sauce and water.
- Cook, stirring, until thickened, about 4 minutes.
- Serve over Chinese Crab Cakes.
- Makes a scant cup of sauce.

Hint: For a quick Chinese hot sauce, mix 2 tbs. Dijon mustard with ¾ c. commercial Sweet and Sour sauce and ¼ c. catsup and a few drops of Tabasco sauce.

ITALIAN SPECIALTIES

CHICKEN CACCIATORI
ITALIAN MEAT SAUCE
SPAGHETTI WITH CLAM SAUCE AND BACON
THICK CRUST PIZZA
VEAL ITALIANO
VEAL PALAZZA

"Serving Spaghetti At A San Francisco Counter Restaurant"

CHICKEN CACCIATORI

2 2-½ to 3 lb. broilers, cut up
2 large yellow onions
2 medium green peppers
3 cloves garlic
2 16 oz. cans tomatoes
1 8 oz. can tomato sauce
½ c. Chianti wine
2 tsp. salt
¾ tsp. pepper
½ tsp. allspice
1 tsp. sugar
2 bay leaves
½ tsp. dried leaf thyme
6 tbs. vegetable oil

- Saute chicken pieces in hot oil, about 10 minutes, in a heavy deep skillet.
- Brown on all sides.
- Remove chicken pieces and keep warm.
- Peel and chop onions to make about 1 cup.
- Wash, remove membranes and seeds from green peppers. Chop to make about ¾ cup.
- Peel and mince garlic.
- Brown onion, green pepper and garlic in the same skillet about 5 minutes.
- Add tomatoes and their juices, wine, salt, pepper, allspice, bay leaves and thyme to sauteed vegetables.
- Simmer vegetables in their sauce about 5 minutes, cutting up tomatoes and stirring well.
- Add browned chicken pieces. Simmer, uncovered, 30 to 40 minutes or until tender. Baste pieces occasionally with sauce.
- Pour sauce over helpings of chicken. Serve with rice.
- Serves 8.

ITALIAN MEAT SAUCE

¼ lb. Mozzarella cheese
1-½ lbs. ground beef
1-½ lbs. Italian pork sausage
2 tbs. olive oil
1 large green pepper
2 large yellow onions
½ lb. mushrooms
1 16 oz. can tomatoes
1 15 oz. can tomato sauce
½ tsp. sugar, ½ tsp. oregano
1 6 oz. can tomato paste

- Remove casing from sausage and slice sausage thin.
- Break apart meat in a large deep skillet.
- Add sausage slices.
- Cook meat over high heat in olive oil until meat has lost its pink color.
- Remove seeds and membrane from green pepper and chop pepper.
- Wash, pat dry and chop mushrooms.
- Peel and chop onions.
- Add onions, mushrooms, green pepper and oregano to meat. Cook 5 minutes.
- Add sugar, tomatoes, tomato sauce and tomato paste. Simmer mixture uncovered until thick, about 1 hour, stirring frequently. Let cool.
- Skim off any surplus grease.
- Use sauce hot over sauteed eggplant slices, (see index) or cooked firm tender cauliflower. Sprinkle grated Mozzarella cheese on top.
- Make a complete meal served with buttered pasta of your choice.

SPAGHETTI WITH CLAM SAUCE AND BACON

6 slices bacon
1 small yellow onion
1 clove garlic
2 tbs. flour
⅔ c. white wine
1 6-½ oz. can chopped clams
¼ tsp. pepper
6 oz. spaghetti
8 parslery sprigs
Parmesan cheese

- Finely dice bacon and cook until almost crisp in a skillet.
- Discard all but 2 tbs. bacon drippings.
- Peel and chop onion.
- Peel and mince garlic.
- Wash parsley, discarding stems. Chop flowerets to make ½ cup.
- Add onion and garlic to bacon and bacon grease in pan. Cook, stirring until vegetables are soft. Stir in flour. Add wine, clams and their liquid. Stir until thick.
- Cook spaghetti in boiling water about 7 minutes. Drain. Do not rinse.
- Put spaghetti back in its cooking pot and pour over the clam sauce. Toss.
- Add parsley.
- Serves 4.
- Serve with Parmesan cheese.

Hint: When cooking spaghetti, use enough water to allow the pasta to dance freely about as it cooks. Add 1 tbs. oil to the boiling salted water to help prevent pasta from boiling over. Rinse in hot water when done to serve immediately.

THICK CRUST PIZZA

This is always made in conjunction with the making of One-Two-Three bread. Only instead of 5 loaves, set aside the fifth portion of dough to use for the pizza crust.

Homemade bread dough (see index)
1 6 oz. can tomato paste
2 tbs. water
½ Peperoni, Italian sausage. About 2 oz.
½ tsp. oregano
½ tsp. basil
¼ c. olive oil
½ tsp. salt
1 medium red onion
1 medium green pepper
½ tsp. sugar
1 2 oz. can sliced black olives
8 fresh mushrooms
12 oz. mozzarella cheese
Freshly ground black pepper

- After it has been kneaded down the second time, roll out the 1/5 portion of bread dough on a floured board with a rolling pin. Roll to about ¼ inch thickness, or as thin as possible. Dough will be springy. If dough resists, let rest 5 minutes to relax gluten, then roll again. Pierce several places with a fork.
- Thin out tomato paste with water. Add dash of sugar.
- Slice peperoni into thin slices. Peel and finely chop the onion.
- Wash, pat dry and slice mushrooms.
- Wash and remove membranes and seed from green pepper. Slice thin crosswise.
- Spread pizza dough with tomato paste. Cover with your choices or all of mushrooms, black olives and cheese. Sprinkle with oregano, pepper and basil.
- Place slices of Italian sausage and slice of green pepper around on pizza.
- Salt and pepper to taste. Add a little more tomato sauce. Pour a little olive oil over the top.
- Let rise in a warm place for 45 minutes or until pizza has risen to about twice its original size.
- Bake at 400 degrees until done, when crust is brown on the edges and cheese is bubbly, about 15 to 20 minutes.
- Cut into squares and serve hot.
- Delicious for hors d'oeuvres, snacks or whenever.

VEAL ITALIANO

1-½ lb. boneless slices of veal, cut ½ inch thick
2 eggs
4 tbs. fine seasoned bread crumbs
2 tbs. butter
2 tbs. salad oil
6 oz. spaghetti
2 8 oz. cans tomato sauce
8 oz. mozzarella cheese
6 tbs. parmesan cheese

- Beat eggs.
- Shred mozzarella cheese.
- Score pieces of veal with a sharp knife on both sides to tenderize.
- Dip veal in eggs and coat on both sides with bread crumbs.
- Fry in a large skillet in butter and oil about 3 minutes on each side.
- Cook spaghetti about 8 minutes in boiling water until tender, but not soft.
- Drain.
- Turn into a large shallow casserole or baking dish.
- Pour half the tomato sauce over the spaghetti and sprinkle with half the cheeses on top. Put sauteed veal on top of spaghetti and cheese.
- Pour other half of tomato sauce over meat, and sprinkle with rest of cheeses.
- Bake, covered, in a 375 degree oven about 15 minutes, until hot and bubbly.
- If using a baking dish, cover it securely with aluminum foil while baking.
- Serves 4.

VEAL PALAZZA

12 serving size pieces sliced veal cutlets (1-½ to 2 lbs.)
12 thin slices ham
12 thin slices swiss cheese
2 tbs. butter
Salt and pepper
½ c. white wine
2 tbs. tomato paste
1 bay leaf
½ tsp. basil

- Cut veal into serving size pieces.
- Top each slice with a slice of ham and a slice of swiss cheese.
- Roll and secure with toothpicks.
- Brown in a large skillet in butter. Salt and pepper to taste.
- Add wine, tomato paste, bay leaf and basil.
- Cover and simmer about 15 minutes until meat is tender. Baste with sauce several times.
- Serves 6.

FISH

CRAB ENCHILADAS, SAN FRANCISCO SPECIAL
CRAB QUICHE
CODFISH CASSEROLE WITH CROUTON TOPPING
CURRIED SHRIMP AND RICE CASSEROLE
SAN FRANCISCO CRAB RAREBIT

Commerical Fishing Boats Tied Up In San Francisco Bay
At Fisherman's Wharf

CRAB ENCHILADA, SAN FRANCISCO SPECIAL

4 corn tortillas
3 tbs. vegetable oil
1 c. crab meat
8 large pieces of crab meat (optional)
1 medium yellow onion
½ lb. jack cheese
Pitted ripe olives
1 avocado
2 medium tomatoes
Sour cream
1 c. fresh salsa (see index) or use a commercial salsa

- Peel and mince onion to make about 4 tbs.
- Peel and slice tomatoes.
- Shred cheese to make about 1-½ cups.
- Dip tortillas in oil heated in a skillet, ½ minute on each side until just soft. Remove with tongs and place on paper towels to drain.
- Place ¼ c. crab meat on each tortilla.
- Sprinkle with 1 tbs. minced onion. Sprinkle with ½ c. cheese.
- Pour a little salsa over each. Roll and place close together in a small shallow baking pan, seam sides down.
- Cover enchiladas with remaining salsa.
- Sprinkle with remaining cheese.
- Bake uncovered at 400 degrees for 10 minutes or until enchiladas are heated through and cheese is bubbly.
- Garnish with olives, slices of avocado and large pieces of crab meat.
- Place a dollop of sour cream on top.
- Serves 2, or 4, if served in combination with rice, beans, or a vegetable.

CRAB QUICHE

½ lb. crab meat
1 9 inch unbaked pie shell (see index for flaky pie crust)
4 eggs
1 c. half-and-half cream and milk
½ tsp. salt
1 4 oz. can sliced mushrooms
1 4 oz. can sliced water chestnuts
1 2 oz. jar pimento pieces
1/8 tsp. pepper
1/8 tsp. ground nutmeg
¼ lb. swiss cheese

- Clean and shred crab, removing all bones and cartilage.
- Beat eggs.
- Grate cheese to make about ½ cup.
- Drain mushrooms.
- Drain water chestnuts.
- Mix eggs, ½ and ½, salt, pepper and nutmeg.
- Sprinkle crab, mushrooms, 2 tbs. sliced water chestnuts and 2 tsp. pimento pieces in pie shell.
- Sprinkle with cheese.
- Pour egg mixture over all.
- Bake at 375 degrees, 35 to 40 minutes, until a knife thrust in center comes out clean.
- Cool on a wire rack.
- Serves 6.

Delicious!

CODFISH CASSEROLE WITH CROUTON TOPPING

1 small yellow onion
¼ c. butter
½ c. flour
2 c. milk
1 tsp. salt
¼ tsp. pepper
1 lb. fresh or frozen codfish
2 tbs. prepared mustard
¼ tsp. dill weed, crushed
1 small lemon
5 medium White Rose potatoes
1-½ c. croutons (see index)
¼ c. melted butter

- Thaw fish, if frozen.
- Cut into bite size pieces.
- Peel and finely chop onion. Peel, cook and cube potatoes into 1 inch cubes.
- Saute onion in a large skillet in butter until golden.
- Add flour, stirring.
- Add milk, continuing to stir until thickened.
- Add salt, dill, lemon juice, pepper and mustard. Stir well.
- Add fish, and potatoes cut into 1 inch cubes, to skillet. Mix and pour into a 2 quart casserole.
- Sprinkle with croutons. Pour melted butter over croutons.
- Bake at 350 degrees about 30 minutes, until bubbly and croutons are crisp and browned.
- Serves 4.

CURRIED SHRIMP AND RICE CASSEROLE

3 tbs. butter
2 c. soft bread crumbs
1 small yellow onion
2-¼ c. milk
3 tbs. flour
1-½ tsp. curry powder, or to taste
½ tsp. salt
1-½ c. cooked rice
1 c. frozen peas
2 c. small shrimp, cleaned and cooked

- Melt butter. Toss crumbs in the melted butter and set aside.
- Cook peas until just tender. Peel and mince onion.
- Saute onions in butter until golden. Stir in flour, curry powder and salt.
- Pour in milk until sauce is smooth, stirring constantly.
- Remove from fire.
- Fold in cooked rice, peas and shrimp.
- Place in casserole. Top with buttered crumbs.
- Bake at 350 degrees about ½ hour until crumbs are golden and contents are bubbly.
- Serves 4.

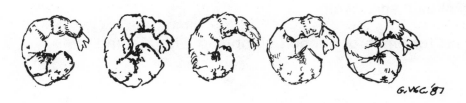

SAN FRANCISCO CRAB RAREBIT

2 tbs. butter
2 tbs. flour
1 c. stale beer
1-½ lb. sharp cheddar cheese
2 eggs
½ tsp. dry mustard
1 tbs. Worcestershire sauce
½ tsp. salt
¼ tsp. pepper
¾ lb. crab meat or 12 crab leg meat sections
French bread (San Francisco, if possible)

- Coarsely grate cheese to make about 2 cups.
- Beat eggs well.
- Melt butter in a large skillet.
- Add flour. Slowly stir in the beer. Stirring. When mixture is thickened and smooth, add the cheese.
- Continue to stir over low heat until cheese is melted.
- Add eggs slowly, stirring until the eggs thicken, but do not over-cook, as eggs will lump.
- Add Worcestershire and salt and pepper to taste.
- Place 2 tbs. crab meat, or 3 crab leg sections on each piece of toast.
- Pour hot rarebit over all immediately and serve on heated plates.
- Makes 4 servings.

A treat for lunch or supper, combined with a salad.

SALADS

PALACE COURT SALAD
STUFFED EGGS
ROQUEFORT STRIPS
CELERY VICTOR SALAD

SALAD DRESSINGS

COURT LOUIS DRESSING
OLD FASHIONED BOILED DRESSING
VICTOR DRESSING

The Court Of The Palace Hotel
Market Street, San Francisco,
Showing Glassed Roofed Court And Dining Room

PALACE COURT SALAD

Anyone who has ever been to San Francisco has seen or heard of the Palace Hotel on Market Street. In the nineteen hundred twenties and thirties, it was at its peak of glory.

Long before then, the immense inner court was an open courtyard, where my mother told of being driven in a horse and surrey, stopping in the center of the inner circle to disembark and enter the hotel.

Years later, the court was covered with a vaulted high glass rotunda. It became an elegant dining room. Huge in dimension, the court was supported by tall marble columns on its outer perimeter. Potted palms surrounded the red velvet carpeted dining area with its red velvet high backed dining chairs and white cloth covered tables, transforming it into a serene and dignified room. It is an unique and distinctive representative of turn-of-the-century elegance. The Palace Court Salad became a trademark of the hotel, and of the city itself.

> ½ **head iceberg lettuce**
> 1 **large tomato**
> 2 **large artichokes**
> ½ **lb. crab meat**
> 6 **crab leg meat sections**
> **French dressing**
> 2 **eggs**
> I **large avocado**
> **Court Louis Dressing (see index)**

- Cook artichokes until tender. Remove leaves and trim hearts. The meaty end of the leaves may be scraped off and used as a vegetable, warmed in butter, or in another salad.
- Hard boil eggs. Cool. Remove shells and mash eggs.
- Shred lettuce. Place a bed of lettuce on 2 cold large salad plates.
- Peel tomato and lay a thick slice in center of each bed of lettuce.
- Top each salad with a large artichoke heart, hollow side up.
- Fill with a tall cone shaped mound of crab meat, marinated in a tart french dressing.
- Ring artichoke and crab with a band of mashed eggs.
- Garnish with crab legs and slices of avocado.
- Top with Court Louis dressing.
- Serves 2.

This is an outstanding salad.

STUFFED EGGS

8 eggs
2 tbs. sweet pickle relish
1 tsp. horseradish
6 tbs. mayonnaise
Paprika
½ tsp. salt
¼ tsp. pepper

- Hard boil the eggs. Cool. Remove shells.
- Cut each in half lengthwise.
- Place yolks in a bowl and whites on a plate.
- Mash yolks with a fork.
- Add salt and pepper to taste.
- Drain as much liquid from pickle relish as possible, and add to yolks, along with horseradish and enough mayonnaise to make mixture spoonable.
- Spoon each white half with a slightly rounded mound of yolk mixture.
- Sprinkle with paprika.
- To add a gourmet touch, minced cooked shrimp may be added to yolk mixture for extra color and taste.

Hint: Best way to hard boil eggs —
Place eggs in a pan covered with cold water.
Bring to a boil and boil 4 minutes.
Remove from heat and let stand at least 15 minutes.
Rinse under cold water. Remove shells when cool. (No unsightly dark line will appear between yolk and white of egg, although that does not harm the taste of the egg.)

ROQUEFORT STRIPS

½ c. (about 4 oz.) roquefort or blue cheese
½ stick butter
3 tsp. Worcestershire sauce
4 celery stalks
Paprika

- Mash cheese and butter in a small bowl. Add Worcestershire sauce to taste until mixture is well blended and of a spreadable consistency.
- Wash and cut celery stalks into 2 inch pieces.
- Spread and fill with cheese mixture.
- Sprinkle each piece with paprika.
- Serves 6.

These are a nice addition to a sandwich lunch, or as an appetizer.

CELERY VICTOR

This salad is identified with Victor's, an old well established restaurant in San Francisco, which is now ensconced on the top floor of the St. Francis Hotel in Union Square. The association is long standing and well deserved.

4 small heads of celery or 2 large ones
1 tsp. salt
4 eggs
2 2 oz. cans flat anchovies
Lettuce

- Hard boil eggs. Cool. Remove shells and mash eggs.
- Drain anchovies.
- Shred enough lettuce for 4 servings.
- Cut off about 5 inches of the celery head bottom, trimming the heart and removing any black markings. Save the rest of the celery tops for other uses.
- Cut the 5 inch lengths in half lengthwise, if using large heads.
- Cover pieces with water in a large pan, and boil until firm tender, about 40 minutes, depending upon the size of the pieces.
- Drain on paper towels. Chill.
- Place celery hearts on bed of shredded lettuce.
- Sprinkle each serving with ¼ of the mashed eggs.
- Arrange 3 or 4 anchovies crosswise over each celery serving.
- Pour Victor dressing (see index) over each serving.
- Serve cold.
- Serves 4.

COURT LOUIS DRESSING

¾ c. mayonnaise
3 tbs. Glad's Chili Sauce (see index) or any commercial
   chili sauce will do
1 small green pepper
¼ c. catsup
2 green onions
¼ tsp. salt
1/8 tsp. freshly ground pepper
2 tbs. chopped sweet pickle

- Wash green pepper. Remove membranes and seeds. Chop to make about 2 tbs.
- Peel and finely chop green onions, using 2 inches of the lower green stems, to make 2 tbs.
- Blend mayonnaise, chili sauce, catsup, green onions, green pepper and pickles. Add salt and pepper and stir well. Let stand at least 1 hour before serving.
- Mix well before serving.
- Serves 4 to 6.

Best for Palace Court Salad. (See index.)

OLD FASHIONED BOILED DRESSING

½ c. sugar
1 c. cream or half and half
1 tbs. butter
2 tbs. prepared mustard
6 eggs
¾ c. vinegar
1 tsp. salt

- In a double boiler over medium heat, mix butter, mustard, sugar and salt together.
- Add eggs, one at a time, stirring well after each egg addition.
- Add cream in a slow stream beating all the while.
- In a separate small pan, heat the vinegar. Add gradually to cream mixture, continuing to mix well.
- Cook in the double boiler until thick, stirring often.
- Pour into a bowl to cool.
- Store in the refrigerator in a covered jar.
- Makes about 1 pint of dressing.
- This is perfect with fruit salad. Keeps well in the refrigerator a week or more.

VICTOR DRESSING

½ c. wine vinegar
¾ tsp. salt
1 tsp. sugar
¼ tsp. coarse black pepper
1-¼ c. olive oil
4 green onions
1 2 oz. jar pimento pieces

- Finely chop pimento to make 3 tsp.
- Peel and finely chop green onions, including 3 inches of their stalks.
- Mix vinegar, salt, sugar, pepper, oil, chopped onions and pimento.
- Pour in a jar with a tightly fitted lid.
- Shake vigorously to blend.
- Store in refrigerator.
- Serve over Celery Victor. (See index.)

CAKES

GOLDEN POUND CAKE
PINEAPPLE UPSIDE DOWN CAKE
POOR MAN'S FRUIT CAKE
PRINCE OF WALES CAKE
SUNDAY MORNING PANCAKES

COOKIES

DAINTY BUTTER COOKIES

DESSERTS

CARROT PUDDING
LEMON SOUFFLE PIE
MAPLE MOUSSE
WINE JELLO
CANDIED WALNUTS

GOLDEN POUND CAKE

½ c. butter
1 c. sugar
5 egg yolks
1 whole egg
1-¾ c. flour
3 tsp. baking powder
⅓ tsp. salt
1 tsp. vanilla
⅔ c. milk

- Cream butter and sugar together.
- Beat egg yolks with 1 egg. Add to creamed mixture. (Save whites for other uses.)
- Mix flour, baking powder and salt. Add alternately with milk to creamed mixture. Beat well.
- Bake 1 hour in a greased loaf pan, 5 x 9 x 2-½ inches, in a slow 325 degree oven until a cake tester thrust into center comes out clean.
- Turn out on a wire rack to cool.
- This cake can be used in so may ways — frosted, under berries or sliced fruit, or just as an accompaniment to ice cream or a rich dessert.

Hint: Egg whites may be kept frozen. Add them to a covered plastic container as you "collect them". 1 cup equals 7 or 8 egg whites.

PINEAPPLE UPSIDE DOWN CAKE

1 c. brown sugar
3 tbs. butter
3 eggs
1-½ c. white sugar
1-½ c. flour
½ c. pineapple juice
1 tsp. vanilla
½ tsp. salt
1-½ tsp. baking powder
6 to 8 pineapple slices
½ c. chopped walnuts, or more if you wish
Whipping cream

- Separate eggs.
- Melt butter in a 10 inch heavy cast iron skillet.
- Sprinkle brown sugar over melted butter.
- Stir in pan until melted, over low heat. Arrange pineapple slices and walnuts in the melted mixture in the skillet.
- Beat yolks well. Gradually add sugar.
- Add pineapple juice, flour, baking powder and vanilla.
- Beat egg whites. Fold into the batter. Pour batter over pineapple slices in pan.
- Bake at 350 degrees, about 45 minutes. For doneness, check by thrusting a cake tester or a broom straw, in center. When tester comes out clean, it is ready to remove from the oven.
- Be careful of the cast iron handle of the skillet. It can get very hot.
- Remove cake from oven and turn over onto a large serving plate, scraping any loose bit of candied sugar from the pan.
- Serve warm with whipping cream.

This is a timeless cake and yet so usable. Everybody likes it. Don't you?

POOR MAN'S FRUIT CAKE

1 c. sugar
1 c. raisins
1 c. chopped mixed candied fruit
1 c. water
½ c. cooking oil
½ tsp. cloves
½ tsp. salt
1 tsp. cinnamon
2 c. flour
1 tsp. soda
½ c. chopped walnuts

- Combine sugar, raisins, candied fruit, water, oil, cloves, salt and cinnamon. Mix well.
- Bring to a boil in a large cooking pot, stirring. Remove from heat. Cool.
- Mix flour and soda. Add this dry mixture to fruit mixture. Stir. Add nuts.
- Pour into a 5 x 9 x 2-½ inch baking pan.
- Bake at 350 degree for about 45 minutes or until a cake tester thrust in center comes out clean.
- Turn out on a wire rack to cool.
- Keeps well.

PRINCE OF WALES CAKE

½ **c. butter**
1-½ **c. brown sugar**
3 **eggs**
2 **tsp. soda**
1 **tbs. hot water**
1 **tsp. each, cloves, allspice, cinnamon and vanilla**
½ **tsp. salt**
2 **c. flour**
1 **c. sour milk**

- Separate eggs. Beat egg yolks. Cream butter and sugar.
- Add beaten yolks to creamed mixture. Save whites for other uses.
- Add soda dissolved in hot water.
- Mix flour, salt, cloves, allspice, cinnamon.
- Add alternately to creamed ingredients, along with vanilla and sour milk.
- Stir well. Pour into 2 greased cake pans or 1 tube pan.
- Bake at 350 degrees about 40 to 45 minutes, or until cake tester thrust into center comes out clean. Baking time may vary. The tube pan takes longer, approximately 55 to 60 minutes.
- If using sweet milk, use 2 tsp. baking powder. Eliminate soda and hot water.
- Mocha frosting goes as well with these layers as it does with applesauce cake, and a frosted tube cake is a thing of beauty. (See index.)

Hint: One teaspoon vinegar added to 1 cup sweet milk, makes sour milk. Stir and let stand 10 minutes. Then proceed with recipe as for sour milk.

SUNDAY MORNING PANCAKES

There is no reason for the name, really. We had these pancakes most often for Sunday morning breakfast, but they are delicious any time.

There are two ways to approach this. The original recipe is very good, but if you are in a hurry, the second works well, also. It's the spreading of the batter in the pan and the cooking that counts.

If you intend to use the easy way, use a good pancake mix according to directions on the box, but add a little more milk, because the batter must be thin to spread easily.

By forming the pan-sized cake, one can lay the thin pancake out on the plate, spread it with buter and your favorite jam, poke the fork in one end and roll it up like a crepe. Make plenty!

3 eggs
4 tsp. sugar
3 tsp. baking powder
1 tsp. salt
1 c. flour
1 c. buttermilk
2 tbs. melted butter
4 tbs. vegetable shortening

- Beat eggs lightly. Add sugar, baking powder and salt.
- Stir. Add flour, buttermilk and melted butter. Stir only until mixed.
- Heat shortening in a large frying pan, about 1 tbs. per pancake. (I prefer an iron skillet for it holds the heat evenly.)
- Spread batter thin by putting about 3 tbs. in center of pan and using the back of the spoon, with a clockwise motion from the center towards the outside, spread until it is almost the size of the pan.
- It's ready to turn with a spatula after numerous small bubbles appear in pancake and it loses some of its gloss.
- Turn your pancakes gently. I've been told that flipping them may be spectacular, but it makes the cakes flat.
- Cook until done, about 3 or 4 minutes on each side, depending upon heat of the pan.
- Keep warm in the oven on an oven proof dish.
- Makes about 8 pancakes.

DAINTY BUTTER COOKIES

½ lb. butter
1-½ c. sugar
2 c. flour
2 eggs
¼ tsp. salt
1 tsp. vanilla

- Beat eggs.
- Cream butter and sugar.
- Add eggs gradually. Beat.
- Add flour and vanilla. Mix well.
- Drop from the tip of a spoon onto a buttered cookie sheet 2 inches apart.
- Spread thin with a wet knife and bake at 325 degrees until nicely browned around the edges, about 8 to 10 minutes.
- Remove with a spatula to paper towels to cool.
- This recipe is best made with "real butter."

CARROT PUDDING

4 or 5 medium carrots
1 c. suet
1 c. dry bread crumbs
1 c. sugar
3 medium apples
2 medium potatoes
1-½ c. raisins
1-½ c. currants
½ c. chopped citron
3 tbs. strawberry jam
1 tsp. each, cinnamon, nutmeg and cloves
1 tsp. baking soda
1 tbs. hot water
2 eggs

- Beat eggs.
- Peel and grate carrots to make 1 cup.
- Chop suet to make 1 cup.
- Peel, core and grate apples to make 1 cup.
- Chop citron into fine pieces to make ½ cup.
- Mix all ingredients except spices and eggs.
- Add spices and eggs last. Beat well.
- Dissolve soda in water. Add to pudding mixture.
- Place pudding in a tightly covered container and steam over simmering hot water 1-½ hours. Add more water for steam, if necessary.
- This is a "substitute" for the original plum pudding recipe from Germany, and is easier to make.
- Serve as one does plum pudding, usually at Christmas time, with hard and soft sauce (see index).

LEMON SOUFFLE PIE

1 baked pie shell (see index under Flaky Pie Crust)
4 eggs
1 scant c. sugar
2 medium lemons
Dash of salt

- Separate eggs.
- Beat egg whites with a dash of salt.
- Beat egg yolks. Add sugar and beat well.
- Add grated rind of 1 lemon and juice of 2 lemons.
- Cook in a double boiler, 8 to 10 minutes, covered, but stirring often, scraping sides of pan to keep well mixed.
- Cook to a custard consistency.
- Remove pan from bottom of double boiler. Fold ¾ of the beaten whites into the lemon mixture.
- Place baked pie shell on an oven proof dish, or a pie plate, and pour in the filling.
- Spread remainder of whites over pie. Broil 3 inches from flame. (Watch carefully, as it browns quickly.) Heat until tops of whites are golden, about 2 minutes. Remove from broiler at once and cool to room temperature to serve.

MAPLE MOUSSE

4 eggs
1 c. maple syrup
1 pint whipping cream

- Separate eggs. Beat yolks.
- Slowly pour maple syrup into the beaten yolks. Continue to beat until well mixed. Heat to almost boiling. Stir. Cool.
- Cook up to almost boiling twice more, cooling between each heating.
- In another bowl, beat egg whites until stiff.
- Whip cream.
- Blend the two white mixtures together.
- Slowly add the cooked syrup mixture, stirring gently but thoroughly until well blended.
- Place in a freezable container and freeze overnight. Stir once or twice during first part of freezing.
- Pour a small amount of maple syrup over each serving.
- Serves 4.

WINE JELLO

1 3 oz. package black cherry jello
1 c. boiling water
½ c. Port wine
½ c. cold water
1 pint whipping cream
2 tsp. sugar

- Place powdered jello in a bowl. Add boiling water. Stir until jello is completely dissolved.
- Let cool 10 minutes.
- Add Port wine and the cold water. Stir. Cover.
- Refrigerate at least 4 hours or until set.
- Whip cream. Add sugar. Whip well.
- Serve in sherbert glasses with whipped cream plopped on top. Or custard sauce (see index) is delicious poured over the top of the jello.
- Serve accompanied by Cinnamon Rounds (see index), or Nutmeg Sugar Cookies (see index).

CANDIED WALNUTS

1 c. brown sugar
¼ c. cream
½ tsp. cinnamon
½ tsp. vanilla
1-½ c. shelled walnut halves

- Mix brown sugar, cream and cinnamon together in a cooking pot.
- Cook to boiling, stirring constantly until a soft ball forms when a bit of the mixture is dropped into cold water, about 12 to 15 minutes.
- Remove from heat and quickly add vanilla and nuts.
- Stir rapidly until mixture can no longer be stirred and coagulates.
- Turn out at once on waxed paper. Separate the nuts while still warm, if the candied sauce holds them together, as they cool.

Section Three

And Then There Is Me!

AND THEN THERE IS ME!

In my own kitchen in Volcano, California, I was staring out of the window at the woods and blue sky above the trees, as usual transfixed for a moment, stopped from the activities I enjoyed there to soak in the peace and quiet that that view always brought to me.

Coming back to the business at hand, "Shucks", I muttered, "I can't remember this recipe. It's been so long. Maybe if I think back — think about my grandmother once again in her high ceilinged kitchen — how did she do it?"

"Let's see", musing out loud, "It was a one, two, three recipe of lard, sugar and salt. Which was the most? Which came first?"

Slowly the picture and the memory appeared. I could see her plop the three tablespoonsful of lard into the large empty wooden bowl.

I reach for the Crisco. "Yes, that's it! Then the sugar and then the salt!"

I had come full circle from my childhood in San Francisco. Born Gladys Worden in ninteen hundred and ten and raised in the City environment, with brief summer vacations in the Sierras, I attended schools there and was graduated from the University of California in Berkeley across the Bay.

After my marriage and raising three children while moving to various places in California and on the West coast of Washington, and back to Sacramento, Long Beach and Santa Barbara in Southern California, Newt and I are now living in the pines in the Sierra Nevada mountains. We enjoy the quiet of the Mother Lode country, today only four hours drive from San Francisco. It used to take my dad two full days to make the trip when we came on vacation a long time ago.

Now, this morning, I was in a typical process that had evolved through the years, referring in memory to my heritage of cooking good food, working out of and on the old recipes.

Just as a song, a melody, can remind one of a place or circumstance, so did these recollections bring back the picture of that first cooking experience and of the food I loved as a child.

As I moved about in that mountain kitchen, I was enveloped in a flood of well being, an awareness of my own satisfied senses, that rush of fulfillment, through the recipes we all have loved and the ways I have learned to prepare them.

AND THEN THERE IS ME! (continued)

Webster defines kitchen, "a room, place or equipment for the preparation and cooking of food". To me, a kitchen can be more than a cooking area. Size and decor are unimportant except as they form a whole that reflects time, circumstance and the personality of the cook. The cooking experience blends with memory, flowing through the kitchen into the recipes being altered and enjoyed there. It is the heart of any home. that is why, having moved many times in the course of my life, the recipes carried with me are closely related in thought and use to the kitchens where they were prepared and where I have absorbed the combination of ingredients and environments.

I recall my galley where I prepared food for two years. Yes, a GALLEY. Newt and I had had a forty four foot ocean-going diesel cruiser built in Tacoma, Washington, in nineteen hundred and sixty five. After taking an unforgettable "shake down" cruise around the San Juan Islands in Washington state and bringing "Starlet" down the western coast of the United States from Canadian waters to Long Beach harbor, California, with a crew of two, we lived aboard for two years on Alamitos Bay, berthed in the Long Beach Yacht Club Marina.

The galley, of course, was compact, including a four burner stove, an oven, sink and serving counter. It even had a spice cabinet that Newt built in a tall eight inch wide supporting column separating the galley and counter from the living salon. I watched sea gulls swooping overhead and heard the soft lapping of the surrounding waters, as I worked there.

There were many visitors aboard. What grandmother could entertain her grandchildren by letting them feed the ever present gulls, or dive off the stern end of her own "back porch?"

The food there was prepared discreetly for lack of space, not inspiration. There could not be much exhuberance of creation, but oh, the joy of living aboard, which influenced every meal and made each one an adventure!

AND THEN THERE IS ME! (continued)

A motto hung over the counter expressed the realities of cooking in a galley.
"Please stay out of my galley,
From my dish washing, cooking and such.
You are kind to have offered to help me,
But thanks, no, thank you so much!
Please don't think me ungracious,
When I ask that you leave me alone,
For my galley's not any too spacious,
And my routine is strictly my own.
Tell you what: You stay out of my galley,
And I promise to stay out of yours!"

From the high ceilinged kitchen of my grandmother's, from the canary there in its cage in the bustling City by the Golden Gate, to the California Jays, Orioles and Red Topped Acorn Woodpeckers carousing through the pine trees outside our windows and on the deck of our mountain home; the flow of good food has followed the trends and customs of three generations and through my lifetime in the kitchens of our own choosing. It is there that I go for relaxation and thought and there the days flow by in sweet content.

I am enjoying the total spectrum of the meaning of food preparation. That's what it is all about. And I love it!

From my grandmother I learned the basis of living. From my mother, the graces of living. Through them both I have gleaned much, which I want to share with you.

Kitchen Window
Volcano, California

121

ABOUT APPETIZERS AND HORS D'OEUVRES

The definition of hors d'oeuvres is "outside of work" and Appetizer means "a bit of something that excites a desire for more." Literally then, we are addressing the making of a tantilizing bit to whet the appetite; a small uncompromising temptation which offers to tempt the indulger with what is to follow, and to compliment a liquid refreshment served before dinner.

Careful selection of the appetizer need not go with the rest of the meal, merely compliment it. One necessarily does not serve fish hors d'oeuvres because one is serving a fish dinner, nor meat balls before dinner planned around beef as a main course.

By custom, identical flavors presented in both the appetizer and the main course is only generally applicable to ethnic dinners: Mexican hors d'oeuvres with a Mexican dinner; chutney dip with an India curry dinner; and the Japanese dinner is sometimes nothing but a series of appetizers all served with an element of surprise and beauty. It is an art in itself.

The following have been personally chosen. They require a comparative minimum of effort in preparation, can usually be made ahead of time and only warmed, or toasted, or cut, at the last minute. They are fun to create and a delight to serve.

ABOUT HERBS, IN PARTICULAR

Herbs, either dried or fresh, enhance ordinary foods. By skillful use, the blandest of dishes, simple soups, stews, vegetables, in fact the whole spectrum of cooked food, may be given added zest, sometimes not by itself, but by subtle combinations of herbs.

One learns by suggestion and personal experiment which herb best accents different foods. Temperance is advised in application and trial by taste, essential. Cold food needs higher seasoning than hot food.

APPETIZERS

AVOCADO APPETIZER
CELERY ROOT DIP
CHINESE DUNKING PORK
COCKTAIL MEAT BALLS
CRAB COCKTAIL
CRAB DELIGHT DIP
CROUTONS
DEVILED HAM TARTS
DIPPING SAUCE
GLAD'S CLAM DIP
HAM AND LIVER PATE
KEPT CHEESE
MARINATED SPROUTS AND MUSHROOMS
STUFFED MUSHROOMS
SCALLOPS CEVICHE
SHRIMP COCKTAIL
SARDINE PATE
SPINACH CHEESE SQUARES
SPROUTS AND WATER CHESTNUTS, MARINATED
NEWT'S FAVORITE CHEESE ROUNDS
JUDY'S TUNA BALLS

AVOCADO APPETIZER

**2 large avocados
1 10-½ oz. can consomme (gelatin added)
3 medium lemons
Salt and pepper to taste**

- Place can of consomme in the refrigerator about 4 hours until jelled.
- Halve, seed, and peel avocados.
- Squeeze lemon juice lightly over avocado meat.
- Place avocado halves on individual small cocktail plates.
- Fill with jellied consomme. Serve with lemon quarters.
- Salt and pepper to taste.
- Serves 4.

Hint: To easily remove the seed from a halved avocado, take a large kitchen knife and slap the blade into the seed until it sticks. Gently twist the knife and the seed will be neatly dislodged.

CELERY ROOT DIP

1 medium celery root
3 to 4 c. water
1 tsp. salt
3 tbs. mayonnaise
1 tsp. Dijon mustard
1 tsp. curry powder
¼ tsp. salt
¼ tsp. pepper

- Scrub and trim celery root. Boil in boiling salted water to cover in a large pot for 45 minutes to 1 hour until fork tender. Add more water if necessary. When tender, drain, peel and mash.
- Stir in mayonnaise, mustard, curry and salt and pepper to taste.
- Beat well. Chill, covered, in refrigerator, at least 8 hours or overnight to allow flavors to mingle.
- Serve as a dip with crackers.

CHINESE DUNKING PORK

How does the Tacoma Narrows Bridge in Washington state span a length of time? How does the sight of it in retrospect lead to a small Chinese restaurant nestled close to its eastern anchor? Because we had enjoyed a delightful dinner for two in the shadow of its suspension arch, many crossings ago.

Because I recall having there a plate of succulent crisply dark edged thinly sliced pork, tender pink in their centers, surrounded by three little bowls containing hot Chinese mustard, a catsupy tomato sauce, and sesame seeds. We recall the bowing waiter graciously indicating that we dip the slices first into the mustard, then the tomato sauce, then the sesame seed. It was a delicious appetizer; a tantilizing taste renewed by our soaring bridge of memory.

> **1 4 lb. boned loin of pork**
> **¾ c. soy sauce**
> **¼ c. sherry wine**
> **1 medium yellow onion**
> **⅓ c. sugar**
> **1/8 tsp. ginger**
> **1 tbs. cinnamon**
> **½ c. sesame seeds**
> **5 tbs. Dijon mustard**
> **3 tbs. catsup**

- Trim excess fat from pork loin. Open it out book fashion.
- Peel and mince onion. Cut meat lengthwise into 4 equal strips.
- Mix soy sauce, sherry, onion, sugar, ginger and cinnamon.
- Place pork strips in a large baking dish. Add marinade and refrigerate 5 hours, turning meat occasionally to cover all sides with the sauce.
- Bake meat in same pan with marinade, about 2 hours at 350 degrees uncovered, until pork is tender inside and crisp on the outside. Baste often.
- Remove meat from pan and cool before slicing thin across the grain.
- To serve, place a dish of sesame seeds, a dish of mustard, and one of catsup on a tray. With fingers, dip a slice of pork first in mustard, then in catsup, and then in the sesame seeds.
- Serves 8 or more. Serve at room temperature.
- Pork slices may be frozen.

COCKTAIL MEAT BALLS

1 lb. ground beef
1 tbs. butter
1 medium yellow onion
1 egg
8 sprigs of parsley
⅔ c. water
¼ c. fine bread crumbs
¼ c. flour
1 tsp. salt
¼ tsp. each, thyme, oregano and pepper
½ c. catsup
¼ c. honey
1 tsp. Dijon mustard

- Beat egg.
- Wash parsley. Discard stems. Chop flowerets to make ½ cup.
- Peel and mince onion.
- Mix beef, onion, egg, parsley, bread crumbs, salt, thyme, oregano, pepper and half the water thoroughly in a mixing bowl.
- Form into balls about 1 inch in diameter.
- Fry on all sides in butter in a large skillet until brown, about 5 minutes.
- Remove and drain on paper towels.
- Add catsup, honey and mustard to skillet. Mix and scrape sides to loosen bits and pieces. Add rest of water. Simmer, covered, about 20 minutes. Stir occasionally and add a little more water if necessary, until thick.
- Serve meatballs warmed in sauce using wooden cocktail picks.
- Serves 6.

CRAB COCKTAIL

⅔ c. catsup
⅓ c. Glad's Chili sauce (see index) or a commercial chili
  sauce
2 tsp. horseradish sauce
1 large lemon
1 small yellow onion
4 sprigs parsley
1 c. white wine
3 drops hot sauce
1 lb. fresh crab meat
1 16 oz. can grapefruit sections
2 medium avocados

- Clean and check crab meat for bones and cartilage.
- Peel and grate onion to make 2 tsp.
- Squeeze lemon to make 3 tbs.
- Wash parsley. Cut off flowerets, discarding stems. Chop to make about ¼ cup.
- Peel and cut avocados into 1 inch pieces.
- Drain grapefruit sections.
- Combine catsup, chili sauce, horseradish, lemon juice, onion, parsley and wine. Mix well. Refrigerate at least 1 hour.
- Arrange crab meat, grapefruit sections and avocado chunks in 6 serving glasses.
- Pour sauce over each. Serve with crackers as an appetizer.

CRAB DELIGHT DIP

1 c. mayonnaise
½ c. sour cream
2 sprigs parsley
1 6-½ oz. can crab meat
1 tbs. sherry
1 small lemon

- Squeeze lemon to make 1 tsp. lemon juice.
- Wash parsley. Discard stems. Chop flowerets to make 1 tbs.
- Shred crab meat, checking for bones or cartilage.
- Combine crab, parsley, sour cream, mayonnaise, sherry and lemon juice.
- Mix well. Chill at least 2 hours, covered, before serving.
- Serve as a dip with crackers.
- Serves 4.

CROUTONS

8 slices white or french bread
Butter
½ tsp. salt, or to taste
2 tsp. Parmesan cheese, or to taste

- Toast and butter bread.
- Cut into ¼ inch squares, removing any tough crusts.
- Place toasted bits in a single layer on a cookie sheet.
- Sprinkle with salt and Parmesan cheese.
- Bake at 375 degrees about 10 minutes, or until golden and well toasted, stirring with a spatula several times to roast evenly. Do not overbrown.
- Cool and store in a covered container.

This is a wonderful and easy appetizer if served hot out of the oven. And a good way to use your left-over slices of breakfast toast. Use on soups, salads, or sprinkled on Glad's Stuffed Bell Peppers (see index) or on Codfish Casserole (see index).

DEVILED HAM TARTS

Flaky Pie Crust dough (see index) (use ½ the dough for 8 to 10 tarts storing the other half, wrapped tightly in plastic wrap. It will keep several days until ready to use)
¼ lb. cheddar cheese
1 8 oz. can deviled ham
½ tsp. Worcestershire sauce
3 small celery stalks

- Finely chop celery to make ¼ cup. Finely grate cheese to make ¼ cup.
- Roll dough into a thin sheet on a floured board. Sprinkle with cheddar cheese and run roller over once more to impress cheese into dough.
- Cut into 3 inch circles.
- Mix ham, celery and Worcestershire sauce.
- Place 1 tsp. ham mixture in center of each round as they are cut and rolled.
- Pull sides of pastry round towards center pinching edges together on top over filling. Prick once or twice with a fork.
- Bake on a cookie sheet for about 15 minutes at 400 degrees until golden.
- Remove to wire rack to cool. Serve warm.
- Makes about 9 tarts.

DIPPING SAUCE

**1 c. orange marmalade (see index) or a commercial
   marmalade
3 tbs. horseradish
3 tsp. Dijon mustard
3 tsp. prepared mustard
1 medium lemon
4 tsp. dry sherry
½ tsp. salt
¼ tsp. pepper**

- Blend marmalade, horseradish, Dijon and prepared mustard, sherry, salt and pepper. Squeeze lemon to make 4 tsp. adding to rest of ingredients.
- Mix all thoroughly.
- Using either large cooked shrimp, small cooked pork sausages, or 1 inch cubes of ham, dip into sauce, using cocktail picks.
- Even ¾ inch slices of frankfurters, turned over in butter, are good dipped in this sauce.

GLAD'S CLAM DIP

1 8 oz. pkg. cream cheese
1 6-½ oz. can chopped clams
½ tsp. onion salt, or to taste
¼ tsp. garlic salt, or to taste
2 tsp. Worcestershire sauce, or to taste
1 small jicama (optional)
Crackers or potato chips

- At room temperature, mash cheese in a mixing bowl with a fork.
- Strain juice from clams, saving juice.
- Add clams to cheese. Mix well. Add Worcestershire sauce and onion and garlic salt to taste.
- Mix well, adding more clam juice for desired dip consistency.
- Peel jicama and cut into strips about 2-½ inches long and ¼ inch wide and thick.
- Serve clam dip with jicama strips for dipping, or crackers or potato chips.
- Serves 4.

This dip may be spread on toasted bread and broiled until bubbly, making a light lunch along with a salad.

HAM AND LIVER PATE

1 4-½ oz. can deviled ham
1 4 oz. can chopped black olives
1 4 oz. can liver spread
½ tsp. vegetable oil
1 small lemon
6 small sweet pickles

- Squeeze lemon to make 1 tbs. juice
- Combine deviled ham with ½ the can of chopped olives in a bowl. Mix.
- Pack into a 1-½ c. oiled mold. A small round bowl will do.
- Combine liver spread with lemon juice and the other half of the chopped olives. Mix well.
- Pack on top of the deviled ham layer. Chill.
- When ready to serve, unmold on a plate.
- Slice sweet pickles crosswise in ¼ inch slices. Press slices in on the inverted meat mold in a covering circular design.
- Serve with crackers.
- Serves 6 to 8.

Left over pate makes a delicious sandwich spread.

KEPT CHEESE

1 lb. sharp cheddar cheese
1 8 oz. pkg. cream cheese
¼ lb. jack cheese
3 tbs. olive oil
2 tsp. dry mustard
½ tsp. onion salt
½ tsp. garlic salt
4 tbs. brandy, or to taste. (More, if Newt mixes it.)

- Finely shred cheddar and jack cheeses.
- Mash cream cheese at room temperature in a large mixing bowl.
- Mix all cheeses together.
- Add olive oil. Mix well. Add mustard, garlic and onion salt.
- Add brandy. Blend all thoroughly until smooth. Taste for flavor.
- Adjust flavors and adding more brandy and oil to reach spreading consistency.
- Pack in a covered crockery container and refrigerate several days before using.
- At least 2 hours before serving, remove from refrigerator. Mix well with a fork at room temperature. Serve with a cheese knife and crackers.
- This can be kept indefinitely, refrigerated, by adding grated portions of any firm cheese and cream cheese, adding seasonings and liquids accordingly in proportion, keeping the balance of flavors.

Delicious spread on 3 inch pieces of celery stalks, with a dash of paprika on top of each for color.

MARINATED SPROUTS AND MUSHROOMS

1 4 oz. can button mushrooms, or ½ lb. fresh mushrooms
2 doz. Brussel sprouts, or 1 pkg. frozen sprouts
½ c. olive oil
¼ c. vinegar
1 large yellow onion
½ tsp. dry mustard
1 tsp. salt
¼ tsp. pepper
3 small bay leaves
2 cloves garlic
3 medium lemons

- If using fresh mushrooms, wash, pat dry and cut in half if too large. Or drain the canned button mushrooms.
- Peel and wash sprouts. Boil 10 minutes, only until firm and tender. Or cook frozen sprouts according to package directions. Drain. Cool sprouts.
- Peel and chop onion to make about 5 tbs.
- Peel and mince garlic.
- Squeeze lemons to make ⅓ cup of juice.
- Combine oil, vinegar, mustard, salt, pepper, bay leaves, garlic, onion and lemon juice. Mix well.
- Pour sauce over sprouts and mushrooms and marinate, covered and refrigerated, for 24 hours.
- Drain and serve with cocktail picks at room temperature.
- Serves 6.

Hint: Sprouts remain green if cooked for a short time. To avoid the cabbage-like cooking aroma, add a stalk or two of celery to the cooking water.

Always cook green vegetables uncovered to retain their green color.

STUFFED MUSHROOMS

2 4-½ oz. cans small shrimp
8 oz. cream cheese
2 green onions
¼ tsp. garlic salt
24 large mushroom caps
¾ c. shelled walnuts

- Drain shrimp.
- Peel and finely chop bottom 3 inches of green onions to make about 2 tbs.
- Mash cream cheese at room temperature and add shrimp, onions and salt.
- Mix well.
- Wash, remove stems (save for other uses) from mushrooms. Pat dry.
- Finely chop walnuts to make ½ cup.
- Stuff mushroom caps with shrimp filling. Sprinkle each cap with chopped walnuts.
- Broil 4 inches below heat until cheese is soft and caps are warm, about 4 minutes.
- Serves 8.

SCOLLOPS CEVICHE

½ c. lime juice
2 lb. fresh scollops
1 medium red onion
3 sprigs parsley
1 bay leaf
1 tsp. oregano
½ tsp. pepper
1 tsp. seasoned salt

- Wash, cut scollops in bite size pieces.
- Peel and chop onion to make ½ cup.
- Chop parsley flowerets to make about 2 tbs., discarding stems.
- Mix well, lime juice, onion, parsley, crumbled bay leaf, oregano, pepper and salt.
- Pour over scollops and marinate, refrigerated and covered, overnight.
- Turn once or twice to thoroughly marinate.
- Drain and serve cold with cocktail picks.
- Serves 6.

SHRIMP COCKTAIL

Here are two ways to serve a shrimp cocktail. One is sweet; the other, spicy. Both are equally delicous. The rest of the menu will determine which is the best choice for you to serve at a particular time.

SPICY VERSION

1 lb. medium cooked shrimp
⅓ c. Glad's Chile sauce (see index), or a commercial chile sauce may be used
1 c. catsup
2 tsp. horseradish sauce, or to taste
3 medium celery stalks
1 medium avocado

- Chop celery fine.
- Peel, seed and cut avocado in ½ inch cubes.
- Mix well the chili sauce, catsup, horseradish to make a spicy sauce.
- Clean shrimp and arrange in cocktail glasses. Mix lightly the celery and avocado cubes and place on top of shrimp. Stir gently.
- Pour sauce over each serving.
- Serve chilled.
- Serves 4.

SWEET VERSION

1 lb. medium cooked shrimp
5 oz. cream cheese
1 15 oz. can pineapple chunks
3 tbs. pineapple juice
½ tsp. ginger
2 tbs. grated coconut

- Drain pineapple chunks, saving 3 tbs. juice.
- Soften cream cheese to room temperature. Mash cheese and gradually add juice to thin to sauce consistency. Add ginger. Mix well.
- Arrange shrimp and pineapple chunks in cocktail glasses.
- Pour dressing over each serving.
- Sprinkle with coconut.
- Chill.
- Serves 4.

SARDINE PATE

3 3-¾ oz. cans sardines packed in olive oil
6 green onions
2 medium lemons
2 eggs
Salt and pepper to taste

- Hard boil eggs. Cool. Peel and finely mash.
- Drain and mash sardines in a mixing bowl.
- Peel and finely mince onions, including about 2 inches of stems.
- Add eggs and onions to sardines and blend well.
- Salt and pepper to taste.
- Add about 2 tbs. lemon juice. Mix well.
- Serves 6 either as an appetizer on toasted rye bread squares, or as a sandwich spread on rye bread.

SPINACH CHEESE SQUARES

½ **cube butter**
3 **eggs**
1 **c. flour**
1 **c. milk**
1 **tsp. salt**
1 **tsp. baking powder**
1 **lb. jack cheese**
2 **bundles fresh spinach**

- Wash spinach, remove stems and chop fine, to make about 4 cups.
- Beat eggs and add milk.
- Mix flour, salt and baking powder. Add to egg mixture. Beat.
- Grate cheese to make about 2 cups.
- Melt butter in a 9 x 13-½ x 2 inch baking dish in the oven.
- Add cheese and spinach to batter and mix well.
- Pour batter into melted butter in pan. Bake 35 minutes at 350 degrees.
- Cool 30 minutes before serving.
- Cut into squares. Serve at room temperature.
- To freeze: place on a cookie sheet and freeze. Then package frozen squares in a freezer bag to store.
- To reheat: place frozen squares in a 325 degree oven on a cookie sheet. Heat 12 to 15 minutes. Serve at room temperature.
- Makes 12 to 16 squares.

It takes extra time and effort to finely chop the fresh spinach, but this is what gives this appetizer the difference in texture and taste.

MARINATED BRUSSEL SPROUTS
AND WATER CHESTNUTS

2 10 oz. pkgs. frozen Brussel sprouts
1 8 oz. can water chestnuts
¼ c. Tarragon vinegar
½ c. salad oil
1 clove garlic
1 tbs. sugar
1 tsp. salt
3 drops hot sauce
4 green onions
1 red bell pepper — or a 2 oz. jar pimento pieces

- Cook sprouts in boiling water until firm tender, according to package directions. Drain and cool.
- Wash, cut membranes out and remove seeds from red pepper. Cut into thin strips. Or drain pimento pieces.
- Thinly slice water chestnuts to make about 1 cup.
- Peel and mince garlic.
- Peel and thinly slice bottom 3 inches of green onions to make about 3 tbs.
- Combine vinegar, oil, garlic, onion, sugar, hot sauce, salt and pepper.
- Mix well. Pour over sprouts and water chestnuts in a large bowl.
- Toss vegetables, cover and chill overnight. Stir once or twice to marinate.
- Drain and serve at room temperature with cocktail picks.
- Serves 6.

NEWT'S FAVORITE CHEESE ROUNDS

16 white or french bread slices
3 large dill pickles
½ lb. sharp cheddar cheese

- Cut bread slices into 2 inch circles with biscuit cutter or top of a small glass. Save rest of slices and crusts for other uses.
- Slice dill pickles crosswise in ¼ inch slices.
- Slice cheese in ¼ inch thick slices and then in approximately 1-½ inch squares to fit on bread circles.
- Toast rounds of bread on one side only in a broiler. Turn and place toasted rounds, toasted side down, on a cool broiler pan. Place a pickle slice on each round. Put a slice of cheese on top of each pickle.
- At this point, these may be covered and kept for several hours until ready to serve.
- Toast in broiler about 6 inches from heat until cheese melts and edges of bread rounds are browned.
- Serve at once, removing with a spatula to a plate.
- Serves 4, estimating 4 to each person.

They disappear quickly.

JUDY'S TUNA BALLS

1 6-½ oz. can tuna
1 tsp. curry powder
2 tbs. chutney
1 8 oz. pkg. cream cheese
Kreutsmeyer Wheat germ, or fine bread crumbs

- Drain and flake tuna.
- Chop chutney.
- Mash cream cheese at room temperature. Add tuna, chutney and curry powder.
- Mix thoroughly. Chill.
- Roll into ¾ inch balls and then roll each in Kreutsmeyer flakes or bread crumbs to cover thoroughly.
- Serve cold with toothpicks.

MEATS

COMPASS ROSE LAMB CHOPS
CORNED BEEF ROLL-UPS WITH THICK AND TANGY TOMATO
    SAUCE
COUNTRY STYLE PORK RIBS
CRANBERRY PORK CHOPS
CURRIED SMOKED PORK CHOPS WITH VEGETABLES
CURRY DINNER FOR SIX
    MENU
    CONDIMENTS
    CHUTNEY DIP
    BEEF CURRY
    FRUIT COOLER
    SHRIMP SAMBAL
    FRIED BANANAS
    CINNAMON ROUNDS
GLAD'S STUFFED BELL PEPPERS
EUGENE OVEN BARBECUED SPARERIBS
GREEN PEPPER STEAK
HAM AND CHEESE TARTS
HAM AND SCALLOPED POTATOES
HAM AND SWEET POTATO CASSEROLE
"HONEY-DO" ROUND STEAK
MUSHROOM STEAKS FOR TWO
OLD FARM PORK CHOPS
OVEN BAKED LAMB CHOPS
PARSLEY LEMON LIVER
PENNSYLVANIA ROAST PORK
PORK CHOPS FLORENTINE
PORK STEAKS AND PARSNIPS
RODEO STEW
SIEMPRE STEW WITH BISCUIT TOPPING
STEAK SAN LUIS OBISPO

COMPASS ROSE LAMB CHOPS

6 ½ inch thick lamb chops
2 tbs. soy sauce
2 tbs. honey
1 tsp. cilantro
1 tsp. ginger
¼ tsp. garlic salt

- Make marinade of soy sauce, honey, cilantro, ginger and garlic salt.
- Mix well.
- Lay chops in a shallow pan and spoon marinade over them. Cover and refrigerate overnight, turning once or twice to coat both sides with sauce.
- Remove chops from marinade. Broil about 4 inches from heat about 6 minutes on each side, basting with marinade, until edges are crusty and brown and chop is done to individual preference.
- Serves 6.

Simply delicious.

CORNED BEEF ROLL-UPS
WITH THICK AND TANGY TOMATO SAUCE

1 medium yellow onion
½ c. flour
1 tsp. baking powder
½ tsp. salt
½ c. yellow cornmeal
½ c. vegetable shortening
½ c. milk
1 12 oz. can corned beef
6 medium White Rose potatoes
Thick and Tangy Tomato sauce (see index)

- Sift flour, baking powder and salt together.
- Stir in cornmeal.
- Cut in shortening to the size of peas.
- Add milk all at once. Mix lightly until dampened.
- Roll out on a floured board into a sheet about 10 x 14 inches and ¼ inch thick.
- Peel potatoes. Boil until just tender. Cool. Dice to make about 2 cups.
- Peel and chop onion to make about 3 tbs.
- Shred corn beef and combine potatoes, meat and onions in a mixing bowl.
- Place mixture down the center of sheet of dough.
- Cut dough in 1 inch strips from meat filling to edge.
- Lace strips of dough together over filling mixture.
- Bake in a 425 degree oven for 20 minutes, until meat is hot and crust is golden. Cut into serving size pieces.
- Serve with Thick and Tangy Tomato sauce spread hot over each slice.
- Serves 4 to 6.

COUNTRY STYLE PORK RIBS

4 lbs. country style pork spareribs
½ tsp. salt
3 tsp. dill seed
¼ tsp. thyme
1/8 tsp. pepper
2 medium yellow onions
1 10 oz. can chicken broth, or 2 chicken bouillon cubes
  and 1-½ c. hot water

- Rub salt and pepper on all sides of ribs. Place in a large casserole in a single layer.
- Sprinkle dill seeds and thyme generously over meat.
- Peel and chop onions and sprinkle over meat.
- Pour undiluted chicken broth over all.
- Bake, covered, in a 350 degree oven until meat is very tender, at least 1-½ hours.
- Baste and check occasionally, adding a bit more liquid, broth or water, if necessary.
- These ribs may be held in a warm oven, covered, until ready to serve.
- Serve with its own clear gravy and parsley potatoes. (See index.)
- Serves 4.

CRANBERRY PORK CHOPS

4 pork chops ¾ inch thick
½ tsp. salt
¼ c. flour
1 tbs. vegetable oil
1 large orange
1 16 oz. can jellied cranberry sauce
1 8-½ oz. can crushed pineapple
¼ c. water

- Grate rind of orange to make 2 tbs.
- Dredge chops in flour.
- Sprinkle salt in skillet and brown chops 15 minutes slowly. (This usually draws out enough fat from the chops to fry them. If they stick, use the vegetable oil to complete the frying.)
- Mix 1 c. cranberry sauce, crushed pineapple with its juices, water and the grated orange rind.
- Pour cranberry mixture over chops in skillet.
- Cover. Simmer 1 hour, until tender, basting occasionally with juices in the pan. Add a bit more water if juices become too thick.
- Serves 4.

CURRIED SMOKED PORK CHOPS WITH VEGETABLES

10 small red potatoes
1 lb. fresh green beans
6 tbs. butter
6 smoked pork chops, ¾ inch thick
2 tbs. whole mustard seeds
2 tsp. curry powder, or to taste

- Scrub potatoes. Boil in their jackets until fork tender, about 15 minutes. Drain.
- Brown chops in a large skillet in 4 tbs. butter, about 8 minutes on each side until meat is tender.
- Keep warm on an oven proof plate in a low oven.
- Stir remaining 2 tbs. butter into skillet. Add mustard seeds and curry. Stir. Add potatoes and brown, stirring until potatoes are cooked and crisp, about 5 minutes. Lift out and keep warm.
- Add cooked beans to pan. Stir to coat with butter and juices.
- Serve potatoes, chop and green beans on each plate, drizzling with any remaining juices left in pan.
- Serves 6.

"India"

153

CURRY DINNER FOR SIX

This dinner has evolved through a personally gathered circle of contacts over a long period of time. We went to our first "India House" curry dinner in San Francisco in the early Fifties. At that time, I hastily jotted down a list of the various condiments we were served and quietly slipped it into my purse. That was the beginning. I also made unforgettable vivid mental pictures of the colorful bowls of condiments, cataloguing for future reference, the attractive presentation and the almost overpowering throaty sharpness of the myriad fragrances emanating from them and from the actual curry itself.

Subsequently, we had "Navy Curry" dinner ideas brought back to us by friends in Navy personnel from overseas, who reported happily that "Navy Curry" had established itself as a looked-forward-to meal at sea. We noted that the condiments were somewhat similar, although not served with the color and glamour that we associate with this dinner and which is part of its charm.

"Curry" may be made with beef, chicken, or lamb. Any good steamed white rice or even instant rice will do. Generally the condiments are served in bright bowls, either placed in the center of the table, forming an attractive centerpiece; passed by an attendant; or served buffet style; depending upon circumstance and size of the guest list. At any rate, hot curry gravy is always offered after each guest has topped his serving of rice and meat with generous helpings of all the condiments. Shrimp Sambal is a dramatic must and fruit cooler a soothing accompaniment.

Imported English Pimm's #1 Cup, the world's first Gin Sling, was invented in eighteen hundred and forty one. Mixed with gingerale or Seven-Up, with a dash of lemon, it is poured over cubed ice and served in frosted mugs. Accompanied by Chutney Dip as an appetizer, it becomes a delightful forerunner for the India Curry dinner. Fried Bananas and Cinnamon Rounds complete the exotic circle.

This is a fun dinner to create and serve. It is a conversational success. Most of the items may be prepared, chopped, mashed and cooked, the day ahead. That makes it easy on the cook. What better recommendation is there?

CURRY DINNER FOR SIX

MENU

APPETIZER	Chutney Dip
MAIN COURSE	Beef Curry and Gravy
	Cooked Rice
	Condiments
	Shrimp Sambal
	Fruit Cooler
DESSERT	Fried Bananas and Cinnamon Rounds
	(see index)

CURRY DINNER FOR SIX

CONDIMENTS

Condiments are served at room temperature in colorful bowls, each with its serving spoon beside it. They are either placed in center of the table as a centerpiece, or on a buffet counter, depending upon the number of people to be served. They may be prepared ahead of time and set out before the guests arrive, each bowl covered with aluminum foil or its own cover. When the beef curry is hot and dinner is to be served, the rice is mounded in the center of the dinner plate, then covered with the meat curry. Each bowl is passed from one guest to another to enable them to spoon its contens on top of the rice and curry, several spoonsful of each condiment. Hot gravy should be passed last to smother the condiments and complete the dish.

RAISINS — Soak in hot water for 15 minutes. Drain. Using half golden raisins and half dark raisins is colorful, but either one alone is fine.

CUCUMBERS — Peeled and chopped. Leave strips of peel, if desired, on cucumber for added color.

CHUTNEY — Any fruit chutney is acceptable. Slightly chop for easier serving.

SWEET PICKLE RELISH — India relish, if obtainable, otherwise any chopped sweet pickle relish will do.

FRIED ONION RINGS — Canned french fried onions are fine.

FRESH LIMES — Cut in quarters. Serve 2 quarters for each individual.

EGGS — Hard boiled. Cooled, shelled and chopped. Serve the yolks in one bowl and the whites in another for added color and variety. They may be chopped together and served in 1 bowl.

BACON — Cut crosswise in small ¼ inch pieces and fried crisp. Drain on paper towels.

PEANUTS — Chopped dry roasted are best.

CURRY DINNER FOR SIX

CHUTNEY DIP

2 8 oz. pkgs. cream cheese
1 12-½ oz. jar chutney of your choice
1 tsp. curry powder, or to taste
1 tsp. ground ginger
Dash of garlic powder
½ tsp. salt
Coarsely ground pepper to taste
1 small yellow onion
2 tbs. brandy, or to taste
2 tbs. rum, or to taste
Slivered almonds

- Peel and finely chop onion to make about 2 tbs.
- Chop chutney.
- Mash cream cheese at room temperature in a mixing bowl.
- Add chutney, curry, ginger, garlic powder, salt, pepper, chopped onion, brandy and rum. Mix all together thoroughly until creamy.
- Mound in a serving dish and sprinkle almonds on top.
- Serve with crisp crackers and a small knife for spreading on crackers.
- May be frozen.
- Serves 8 to 12.

CURRY DINNER FOR SIX

BEEF CURRY

3 lb lean beef stew or round steak cut ¾ inch thick
3 tbs. vegetable oil
2 medium yellow onions
1-½ c. beef broth
3 tsp. curry powder, or to taste
1 clove garlic
¼ tsp. chili powder
2 tbs. soy sauce
2 tbs. flour
2 tbs. water

- Peel and chop garlic and onions.
- Cut meat in ½ to ¾ inch cubes. Fry in oil in a large skillet or dutch oven until brown and half of the juice has evaporated.
- Remvoe meat from pan with a slotted spoon after browning for 10 minutes.
- Add onion, curry, garlic and chili powder to pot. Cook until onion is limp, about 5 minutes.
- Return meat to pan. Stir in broth and soy sauce.
- More gravy may be made by adding another cup of water and another cup of broth. Add more seasonings in proportion.
- Meat should be very tender, and gravy only slightly thick.
- Serves 6.

This curry may also be made, using chicken or lamb, substituting chicken broth for beef broth in the recipe.

CURRY DINNER FOR SIX

FRUIT COOLER

1 20 oz. can pineapple chunks
1 16 oz. can whole cranberry sauce
3 bananas
1 pkg. frozen strawberries
3 tbs. sherry wine, or to taste
Fresh seedless Thompson grapes, if available
1 11 oz. can mandarin oranges

- Drain pineapple, saving juice.
- Drain mandarin oranges.
- Mix pineapple, oranges and cranberry sauce ahead of time, if desired.
- Before serving, add thawed strawberries with their juice, and grapes.
- Stir in Sherry wine and mix gently. If a little more juice is needed, use some of the pineapple juice. Slice bananas last and add to fruit cooler.
- Served at room temperature in individual bowls to each guest, along with the main course.
- Serves 6 to 8.

CURRY DINNER FOR SIX

SHRIMP SAMBAL

1 tbs. peanut oil
2 small hot dried red chile peppers
3 tbs. chunky peanut butter
1 large yellow onion
1 lb. cooked medium shrimp
1 tsp. sugar
4 tbs. water

- Remove seed and chop dried peppers very fine.
- Peel and thinly slice onion.
- Heat oil in a large skillet. Fry onion about 5 minutes until the rings are limp.
- Add chopped peppers and water. Stir.
- Stir in peanut butter over low heat. Add salt and sugar.
- Stir and cook 2 minutes. Add shrimp. Blend well, simmering another 2 or 3 minutes to coat with sauce.
- Cool and serve at room temperature in a large shallow serving dish, to be placed by each guest either on his beef curry, rice and condiments, or along the side.
- Serves 6.

Hint: Shrimp Sambal may be served as a surprising appetizer. Just spread it on crackers or toasted bread squares.

CURRY DINNER FOR SIX

FRIED BANANAS

4 large ripe bananas
4 fresh limes
Powdered sugar
Cinnamon
8 tbs. butter
Salt water

- Make saline solution of ½ tsp. salt to 2 c. water in a bowl.
- Peel bananas and cut in half and then again in half lengthwise to make 16 quarters. Drop quarters in saline solution until all are cut.
- Remove at once and drain on paper towels.
- Melt butter (approximately 1 melted tsp. per banana piece), in a large skillet. Fry banana pieces until golden, about 5 minutes, depending upon firmness of banana.
- While frying over low to medium heat, sprinkle with sugar and cinnamon. Squeeze lime juice on each piece. Turn with a spatula and repeat the process.
- Remove carefully with a spatula to a serving plate, when coated and golden. Cool.
- Serve cold, with Cinnamon Rounds (see index) as a dessert.

CURRY DINNER FOR SIX

CINNAMON ROUNDS

Flaky Pie Crust dough (see index)
Cinnamon, about 5 or 6 tbs.
Sugar, about 5 or 6 tbs.
Butter, about 5 tbs.

- Roll enough dough out on a floured board to make a long piece about 10 x 16 inches and ¼ inch thick. Use rest of dough for another roll of Cinnamon Rounds, or save for other uses, wrapped tightly in plastic wrap in the refrigerator.
- Sprinkle generously with sugar and cinnamon.
- Add dollops of butter over all about 2-½ inches apart.
- Roll by hand, starting with the 16 inch end, into a tight roll, tucking butter pieces, sugar and cinnamon into the roll as you go.
- Leaving long roll with seam side down, slice into 1 inch rounds, crosswise.
- Stand rounds upright, about 1 inch apart, on a greased cookie sheet.
- Bake about 20 minutes at 350 degrees until golden.
- Makes 16 rounds.

GLAD'S STUFFED BELL PEPPERS

1 medium yellow onion
2 tbs. bacon grease
1 lb. ground beef
4 inch piece smoked sausage
3 cups water
1 c. cooked Wild and Brown rice, or 1 c. instant brown rice
2 large green or red bell peppers
4 tbs. Glad's Chili sauce (see index) or commercial chili
  sauce
6 tbs. water
4 tsp. butter
½ tsp. basil
¼ tsp. marjoram
¼ tsp. oregano
½ tsp. salt
¼ tsp. pepper
½ c. croutons (see index)

- Cut peppers in half lengthwise. Remove membranes and seeds.
- Cook in boiling water about 5 minutes until just crisp tender. Drain.
- Cook rice according to package instructions.
- Peel and finely chop onion. Saute in a large skillet in butter until golden.
- Add crumbled beef, basil, marjoram, oregano, salt and pepper. Fry, stirring, until meat is brown and most of juices are absorbed, about 6 minutes.
- Simmer sausage piece in 3 tbs. hot water in a small frying pan until water is evaporated and meat just begins to brown, about 6 minutes. Cool. Peel. Chop sausage. Add to browned meat.
- Add cooked rice and chili sauce, mixing well.
- Fill pepper halves to overflowing with meat and rice mixture.
- Place stuffed peppers in a baking dish, meat side up.
- Add a little water to baking pan to help prevent sticking. Dab a tsp. of butter on top of each pepper half.
- Press croutons over top of each stuffed pepper to cover.
- Bake uncovered in a 350 degree oven until butter is melted and peppers are hot, about 30 minutes.
- Serve with brown gravy, if available, or more Chili Sauce.

EUGENE OVEN BARBECUED SPARERIBS

4 lbs. pork ribs, cut into serving size pieces
2 medium lemons
2 medium onions
1 8-½ oz can crushed pineapple
4 tsp. steak sauce
1 tsp. soy sauce
1 tbs. catsup
1 8 oz. can tomato sauce
2 c. water

- Peel and thinly slice onions.
- Slice unpeeled lemons.
- Place ribs in a shallow large baking pan, meaty side up. On each piece place a slice of unpeeled lemon and a slice of onion.
- Bake at 425 degrees about 30 minutes.
- While baking, combine steak sauce, soy sauce, catsup, tomato sauce and water. Pour over ribs.
- After ribs have baked ½ hour, turn oven to 325 degrees and bake 45 minutes to 1 hour longer.
- Baste often and turn once or twice until ribs are crusty.
- Serves 6 or 8.

This wonderfully thick sauce may be used later to spread over hamburgers, in stew, or poured over noodles for a quick lunch.

GREEN PEPPER STEAK

1 large T-Bone steak cut ½ inch thick
1 tsp. cornstarch
1 tsp. soy sauce
1 tsp. peanut oil
1 tbs. white wine
2 cloves garlic
1 medium red or yellow onion
2 medium green peppers
4 tbs. peanut oil
¼ tsp. salt
1 tsp. cornstarch
½ c. water
1 tsp. soy sauce
½ tsp. sugar

- Peel and mince clove of garlic.
- Mix cornstarch, soy sauce, oil, wine and garlic to make a marinade.
- Cut steak from bone. Cut meat into ¼ inch wide strips, about 3 inches long.
- Marinate steak strips for at least 2 hours, turning occasionally to thoroughly coat.
- Peel and thinly slice onions.
- Peel and mince other clove of garlic.
- Remove membranes and seeds from green pepper and cut into thin strips.
- Stir fry steak strips in oil in a large skillet for 4 minutes, until browned and glazed.
- Remove meat to an oven proof plate to keep warm in a low oven.
- Add rest of peanut oil to skillet.
- Stir fry onions and green pepper only until slightly cooked, about 1 minute.
- Add steak strips, salt, garlic, cornstarch, water, soy sauce and sugar.
- Stir fry 2 minutes until vegetables are crisp tender and glazed and meat is hot.
- Serve immediately over Chinese rice (see index).
- Serves 2 generously.

HAM AND CHEESE TARTS

Flaky Pie Crust dough (see index)
1 large yellow onion
¼ lb. fresh mushrooms
2 tbs. butter
½ lb. cooked ham
1 tbs. Dijon mustard
4 sprigs parsley
3 eggs
⅔ c. milk
1 lb. sharp Cheddar cheese
6 foil tart pans

- Roll pastry dough on a floured board to a ¼ inch thick sheet. Cut into 8 inch circles.
- Fit into greased 6 inch diameter pie pans.
- Bake at 350 degrees 25 minutes, until golden. Cool in their pans on wire racks.
- Shred cheese to make 2 cups. Dice cooked ham.
- Wash, pat dry and slice mushrooms.
- Chop parsley flowerets to make ⅓ cup, discarding stems.
- Peel and chop onion.
- Saute onion and mushrooms in butter until limp, about 5 minutes.
- Add diced cooked ham and cook until juices evaporate.
- Stir in mustard and parsley.
- Beat eggs with milk. Add shredded cheese. Stir into ham mixture.
- Pour into baked pastry lined pans.
- Bake at 350 degrees for 30 minutes or until set when knife inserted in center comes out clean.
- Each 6 inch pan serves 2.

This filling may also be baked in a baked pie shell instead of individual tarts, or smaller 4 inch individual tarts, each serving one.

HAM AND SCALLOPED POTATOES

4 medium White Rose potatoes
2 medium carrots
1 medium yellow onion
1 11 oz. can chicken broth
½ c. milk
1 tbs. flour
1 tbs. water
¼ tsp. salt
1/8 tsp. pepper
½ cube butter
1 large ½ inch thick slice cooked baked ham
¼ lb. cheddar cheese

- Peel potatoes. Slice thin and reserve in a bowl of water.
- Peel carrots and slice thin. Hold in same bowl of water to preserve crispness and color.
- Peel and slice onion, breaking slices into rings. Set aside.
- Remove any fat from ham and cut slice into serving size piecs.
- Grate cheese to make about ½ cup.
- Mix undiluted chicken broth, milk, salt and pepper. Add cheese. Heat until cheese is melted. Do not boil.
- Mix flour and water and add gradually to hot broth and cheese mixture.
- Stir and cook until slightly thick.
- Place ½ of sliced potatoes on bottom of a 1-½ qt. greased casserole.
- Put ham pieces on top of the potatoes, then a layer of onions and a layer of carrots. Cover with rest of potatoes. Dot with butter.
- Pour cheese sauce over all.
- Bake covered at 400 degrees for ½ hour. Then reduce temperature to 350 degrees and bake, uncovered, until done, approximately ½ hour. Test by inserting fork into contents of casserole.
- Serves 2 generously.

HAM AND SWEET POTATO CASSEROLE

4 medium sweet potatoes
1 16 oz. can sliced pineapple
½ c. brown sugar
2 tsp. dry mustard
1 slice cooked ham cut ½ inch to 1 inch thick

- Peel sweet potatoes. Cut into ¼ inch slices crosswise.
- Drain pineapple. Combine ½ c. pineapple juice, sugar and mustard, mixing well.
- Arrange sweet potato slices and all but 2 slices of pineapple in a buttered 2 qt. casserole, in alternate layers. Spread ½ pineapple syrup mixture on top.
- Cut ham into serving size pieces and lay on top of contents of casserole.
- Arrange remaining pineapple slices on top of ham.
- Spread remaining pineapple syrup mixture over ham pieces.
- Bake, covered, in a moderate oven, at 350 degrees, for about 1 hour, or until potatoes are cooked.
- Serves 4.

"HONEY-DO" ROUND STEAK

3 lbs. round steak, cut ¾ inch thick
3 tbs. vegetable oil
¼ c. flour
½ tsp. salt
¼ tsp. pepper
2 tbs. horseradish
3 tsp. honey
1 tbs. butter
1 11 oz. can mushroom soup
1 5 oz. can evaporated milk
1 8 oz. can sliced mushrooms

- Cut steak into serving size pieces.
- Sprinkle with flour, salt and pepper.
- Brown steak in a large skillet in oil, about 3 minutes each side.
- Arrange in a 3 qt. baking dish.
- Spread with horseradish and honey.
- Add remaining flour to skillet and blend in undiluted soup, evaporated milk and mushrooms, including their liquid.
- Stir and cook over medium heat 3 minutes, until well blended.
- Pour over meat. Cover.
- Bake at 350 degrees about 1-½ hours. Check on consistency of gravy and add a little water if needed, while baking.
- Serves 6.

MUSHROOM STEAKS FOR TWO

½ lb. fresh mushrooms
2 beef cubed steaks
1 tbs. flour
¼ tsp. salt
Dash of ground pepper
2 tbs. butter
¾ tbs. prepared mustard
1 tbs. Worcestershire sauce
1 small yellow onion
1 10-½ oz. can beef bouillon

- Rinse, pat dry and slice mushrooms.
- Peel and chop onion to make about 2 tbs.
- Dredge both sides of steaks with flour, salt and pepper.
- Brown steaks in butter over high heat, 1 minute on each side.
- Remove from pan to a plate.
- Spread both sides of steaks with mustard and sprinkle with Worcestershire sauce. Keep aside on plate.
- In same skillet, saute mushrooms and onion for 2 minutes.
- Stir in ½ c. bouillon, a bit more Worcestershire sauce, adding any juice accumulated in the holding plate.
- Reheat steaks in hot sauce 3 or 4 minutes. Serve with mushroom juices.
- Serves 2.

Hint: To freeze mushrooms, (particularly during the season when mushrooms are plentiful and the least expensive) — Wash mushrooms. Pat dry. Cut in slices, or if small buttons, keep whole. Saute about 1-½ cup sliced mushrooms at a time, until golden, about 5 minutes. Before juices have evaporated, place sauteed mushrooms in a freezer bag, with their buttered juices. Freeze.

OLD FARM PORK CHOPS

3 medium carrots
3 stalks celery
6 pork chops ¾ inch thick
2 tbs. bacon grease
¾ tsp. salt
½ tsp. pepper
¾ c. water
1 medium yellow onion
2 tbs. prepared mustard
2 tsp. Worcestershire sauce

- Brown chops in bacon drippings 8 minutes each side, 3 at a time, if necessary. Remove chops from pan as done until all are browned. Keep warm on an oven proof plate in a low oven.
- Peel and chop onion.
- Peel and finely dice carrots to make about ½ cup.
- Finely chop celery to make ½ cup.
- Sprinkle onion, carrots and celery in a 2-½ qt. buttered casserole.
- Salt and pepper to taste. Add chops, lapping over each other, if necessary.
- Mix mustard, Worcestershire sauce and water. Add to frying pan. Cook to blend about 3 minutes, scraping all bits and pieces in pan.
- Pour juices over chops and vegetables in casserole.
- Bake, covered, at 350 degrees, 1 hour until tender.
- Serve with baked sweet potatoes, applesauce and a green vegetable
- Serves 6.

This recipe works equally as well using the shorter and thicker country cut pork ribs.

OVEN BAKED LAMB CHOPS

⅓ c. melted butter
6 arm shoulder (round bone) lamb chops
4 tbs. butter
3 medium yellow onions
1 clove garlic
½ tsp. salt
¼ tsp. pepper
1 11 oz. can chicken broth
1 tbs. dried parsley
4 whole cloves
4 large White Rose potatoes, about 1 lb.

- Peel and chop onions.
- Peel and mince garlic.
- Peel and thinly slice potatoes. (Hold in a bowl of water until ready to use.)
- Cut as much fat as possible off of the chops. Brown chops in butter in a large skillet. Remove from the pan to an oven proof plate and keep chops warm in a low oven.
- Saute onion and garlic in same chop skillet until soft, about 5 minutes, adding a bit more butter if needed. Set aside.
- Place slices of potatoes in a buttered baking dish. Add salt and pepper.
- Place chops on top of the potato slices.
- Sprinkle sauteed onions and garlic over contents of caserole.
- Bake in a 375 degree oven, uncovered, until potatoes are golden and tender.
- Test with fork for doneness after about ¾ hour. Bake half hour longer at 325 degrees.
- Serves 2 generously.

PARSLEY LEMON LIVER

6 thin slices baby beef or calf liver
½ tsp. garlic salt
¼ tsp. pepper
¼ lb. (1 cube) butter
2 medium lemons
6 to 8 fresh parsley sprigs

- Rinse liver pieces, cutting out any large membranes. Drain.
- Wash parsley, remove stems and chop flowerets to make about ¼ cup.
- Squeeze lemons to make 4 tbs. juice.
- Cut drained meat into 1 inch wide strips. Sprinkle with garlic salt and pepper.
- Saute strips in butter sizzling hot but not brown, for 2 minutes. Stir to brown all sides. Butter will brown as liver is cooking.
- Remove strips of liver from pan.
- Add lemon juice and parsley to browned butter. Heat, stirring, and pour over liver.
- Serve immediately with rice or noodles.

PENNSYLVANIA ROAST PORK

1 4 to 5 lb. boned and rolled pork roast, or a 4 to 5 lb. rib end of pork
1 clove garlic
1 tsp. rosemary
1 tsp. salt
2 c. brown sugar
½ c. vinegar
1 small hot red pepper
½ c. cold water

- Preheat oven to 450 degrees.
- Peel and mince garlic.
- Seed and crush dried red pepper.
- Sprinkle roast with garlic, rosemary, salt and red pepper.
- Place roast, fat side up, in a Dutch oven.
- Bake, uncovered, 15 minutes at 450 degrees.
- Put the brown sugar in a deep frying pan. Cook over very low heat until sugar melts and starts to carmelize. Stir while cooking. Do not let sugar burn.
- Warm vinegar and stir slowly into melted brown sugar.
- Reduce oven to 300 degrees after baking for 15 minutes at 450 degrees.
- Pour off fat if any has accumulated from pork.
- Pour water into Dutch oven around roast.
- Baste the meat with the vinegar and sugar mixture.
- Bake, covered, basting frequently, about 2 hours, or until pork is very tender. Serve sliced.
- Spoon off excess fat from liquid in Dutch oven and serve sauce separately.
- Serves 6.

If there are any juices left, pour into a bowl and chill in refrigerator. Grease will coagulate on top and will be easily removed. Left over pork is delicious sliced and warmed in the juices. Serve with parsley potatoes or wide noodles, and a green vegetable.

PORK CHOPS FLORENTINE

8 **loin pork chops ½ inch thick**
4 **pkgs. frozen leaf spinach**
9 **tbs. butter**
2 **tbs. flour**
1-½ **c. milk**
1 **tsp. seasoned salt**
¼ **tsp. pepper**
¾ **lb. sharp cheddar cheese**

- Grate cheese to make 1 cup.
- Cook spinach according to package directions. Drain well.
- Brown chops in ½ the butter, 4 at a time in a large frying pan, about 8 minutes each side.
- Sprinkle with seasoned salt.
- After frying, keep warm on an oven proof plate in a low oven.
- Melt the rest of the butter in the same frying pan.
- Stir in the four. Add milk, stirring to make a smooth sauce and scraping bits and pieces from sides and bottom of pan.
- Add pepper and more salt to taste. Add cheese and cook until cheese is melted and sauce is thickened and smooth.
- Combine spinach and cheese sauce, folding spinach into sauce to mix well.
- Pour into a 3 qt. casserole.
- Arrange browned chops on top of spinach, and adding any juices that have gathered in the oven proof plate.
- You may use 2 1-½ qt. casseroles, dividing spinach and chops in each, overlapping the chops to fit.
- Casseroles may be covered and refrigerated to as long as 8 hours at this point before baking.
- Bake, covered, in a 350 degree oven about 60 minutes, or unitl chops are tender. Then uncover and bake 15 minutes more.
- Serves 8.

(See "Menu" in index, for complete dinner.)

PORK STEAKS AND PARSNIPS

6 pork steaks, ½ inch thick
2 tbs. bacon grease
¾ tsp. salt
¼ tsp. pepper
8 medium parsnips
1 11 oz. can mushroom soup

- Cut surplus fat off of steaks and brown in a large skillet in bacon grease about 8 minutes each side.
- Season with salt and pepper.
- Peel parsnips and cut into 3 inch strips, about ½ inch wide.
- Arrange around steaks in skillet.
- Spread undiluted mushroom soup over steaks and parsnips.
- Cover pan tightly. Simmer about 45 minutes, or until meat and vegetables are tender. Add a little water during cooking to prevent burning.
- Serves 6.

RODEO STEW

2 lb. round steak cut about ¾ inch thick
½ c. soy sauce
2 tbs. bacon drippings
4 c. boiling water
1 large yellow onion
1 tsp. Worcestershire sauce
1 tsp. garlic powder
1 tsp. salt
1 tsp. brown sugar
4 medium potatoes
6 medium carrots
1 pkg. frozen string beans
8 small white onions
2 tbs. flour
¼ c. cold water

- Cut steak into 1 inch cubes.
- Marinate meat cubes in soy sauce 1 hour, turning once or twice to cover thoroughly.
- Peel and chop onion to make about ½ cup.
- Peel and slice carrots to ¼ inch slices crosswise.
- Peel small white onions.
- Brown meat cubes in bacon fat in a large deep skillet or pot.
- Add water, Worcestershire sauce, garlic powder, chopped onion, salt and sugar.
- Cover. Simmer 1-½ hours, or until tender.
- Peel and cut potatoes into 1 inch cubes.
- Add string beans, small onions and carrots to stew. Cook 10 minutes.
- Add potatoes and cook 25 to 30 minutes longer until all vegetables are very tender.
- Thicken stew with flour mixed with cold water.
- Delicious served with biscuits.
- Serves 6.

SIEMPRE STEW WITH BISCUIT TOPPING

1 large T-Bone steak cut ½ inch thick
2 tbs. bacon drippings
1 medium yellow onion
1 c. water
2 large celery stalks
1 medium carrot
¼ head of a medium cabbage
1 large White Rose potato
½ tsp. salt
¼ tsp. pepper
1 bay leaf
½ tsp. sage
1 medium tomato
1 4 oz. can sliced mushrooms
1 c. Bisquick
¼ c. water

- Cut meat off bone in ½ inch pieces. Remove most of fat. Save bone.
- Peel and chop onion. Saute onion in bacon drippings in a large deep skillet until soft and golden, about 5 minutes.
- Add meat pieces and fry until brown on all sides. Add salt and pepper.
- Add sage and bay leaf. Add bone.
- Pour water over contents in skillet. Simmer 1 hour, covered, until tender, stirring occasionally. Add a little more water if stew becomes too dry.
- Meanwhile, peel carrots and cut into ½ inch pieces crosswise.
- Cut celery stalks into ½ inch pieces.
- Peel tomato and cut into ½ inch pieces.
- Chop cabbage. Drain mushrooms.
- Add carrots and celery to simmering meat. Stir. Simmer for ½ hour until vegetables are tender. Add more water if necessary. Stew should be rather thick. Remove bone. Add potatoes, tomato, and mushrooms and cook 10 minutes.
- Pour into a 1-½ qt. casserole.
- Bake in a 350 degree oven, covered, for 20 minutes, until bubbly.
- Make a drop biscuit dough from Bisquick and water. (Makes 4 biscuits.)
- Uncover casserole and drop dough by tbs. on top of bubbling stew.
- Bake about 25 minutes longer, uncovered, until biscuit topping is baked and golden brown.
- Serves 2 generously.

This stew may also be made with left over pot roast, omitting the necessity of cooking the meat until tender first.

STEAK SAN LUIS OBISPO

1 small eggplant
1 egg
½ tsp. salt
½ c. dry bread crumbs
4 tbs. butter
4 small cubed steaks or thinly sliced Spencer steaks
Smoked salt to taste
1 7 oz. can whole green chiles
4 ½ inch thick serving size slices of cooked ham
1 tsp. butter
4 serving size slices of Swiss cheese

- Cut off ends, peel and slice eggplant in thin slices crosswise.
- Salt slices and sprinkle with water. Hold in a bowl until ready to fry.
- Beat egg in a shallow dish.
- Dip eggplant slices in egg, carefully covering both sides. Sprinkle with dry bread crumbs.
- Fry in butter in a single layer in a large skillet, about 4 minutes each side, or until golden and crisp outside and fork tender inside. Remove slices and keep warm on an oven proof plate in a low oven until all are cooked.
- (Extra slices may be stored in refrigerator and rewarmed to be served as a vegetable at another time.)
- Drain chiles. Open out, rinse and remove seeds.
- Fry ham in butter about 2 minutes each side. Keep warm.
- Sprinkle meat with smoked salt. Fry in butter, one minute each side for rare, or 2 minutes for medium. The Spencer steaks will take a little longer than the cubed steaks.
- Place the 4 largest eggplant slices on a broiler pan. Layer each with a steak, then, in succession, a chile slice, ham slice and cheese slice.
- Secure with wooden picks to prevent sliding.
- Broil the 4 stacks about 4 inches from the heat until cheese is bubbly and stacks are hot.
- Serve at once, lifting each stack carefully with a spatula to the individual serving plates.
- Serves 4.

Good in combination with Gypsy Hominy. (See index.)

POULTRY

BAKED CHICKEN CROQUETTES
DIJON BROILED DRUMSTICKS
EASY BAKED CHICKEN
"SO LONG" TURKEY

BAKED CHICKEN CROQUETTES

3 fresh chicken breasts, or left over chicken chopped to make 2 cups of cooked chicken
3 tbs. chicken broth, or 1 chicken cube dissolved in 3 tbs. hot water
½ c. mayonnaise
2 medium celery stalks
½ tsp. salt
1 small yellow onion
1 c. soft bread crumbs
¼ c. dry bread crumbs

- Chop or run through a meat grinder enough cooked chicken meat to make 2 cups.
- If using fresh chicken breasts, fold securely in aluminum foil, leaving a little air space for steam to gather under top folded seam.
- Bake about 1 hour in a 350 degree oven or until fork tender.
- Be careful of steam. Open foil at top seam to test. Save gathered juice for other uses.
- Cool. Remove meat from bones. Discard bones and skin.
- More breasts may be baked at one time, and extra meat frozen for future use.
- Finely chop celery to make 2 tsp.
- Mix mayonnaise with salt, onion and celery. Stir broth slowly into mayonnaise mixture.
- Add chopped chicken and soft bread crumbs. Mix well.
- Shape into pyramids about 2 inches wide at the bottom and 2 inches tall.
- Cover well with bread crumbs on all sides.
- Stand in a shallow baking pan.
- Bake at 450 degrees 15 to 20 minutes until crisp and light brown.
- Serve with chicken gravy and Orange Cranberry Sauce. (See index.)
- Makes 6 croquettes.

DIJON BROILED DRUMSTICKS

8 chicken drumsticks
5 tbs. Dijon mustard
1 c. dry bread crumbs
5 tbs. butter

- Place chicken legs in a large piece of aluminum foil, folding it over securely to make a juice-tight package. Bake about ½ to ¾ hour, depending upon size of drumsticks, until legs are fork tender. Save foil-collected juices for other uses.
- Remove legs from foil and mark skin in diamond pattern with a sharp knife. Spread each drumstick generously with mustard on all sides.
- Roll in bread crumbs.
- These may be kept, covered, in refrigerator until 15 minutes before serving time. Then melt butter, and pour over drumsticks, rolling to cover thoroughly.
- Broil 4 inches below heat, about 15 minutes, turning with tongs to brown evenly. Remove to an oven proof plate in a low oven until ready to serve.
- Serves 4.

Good either hot or cold. Great in a picnic lunch.

EASY BAKED CHICKEN

3 to 3-½ lb frying chicken, cut up
¼ c. flour
¼ c. melted butter
1 5 oz. can evaporated milk
1 10-½ oz. can cream of mushroom soup
½ lb. cheddar cheese
1 tsp. salt
½ tsp. pepper
3 stalks celery
1 16 oz. can small white onions
¼ lb. fresh mushrooms
Paprika

- Coat chicken pieces in flour.
- Melt butter and pour into a large baking pan.
- Arrange chicken in a single layer in the pan, skin side down.
- Bake, uncovered, at 425 degrees for 30 minutes. Turn pieces. Bake 25 minutes more or until brown and tender.
- Remove pan from oven.
- Grate cheese to make 1 cup.
- Chop celery fine to make ½ cup.
- Drain onions and discard any tough outer skins.
- Wash, pat dry and slice mushrooms.
- Sprinkle mushrooms, onions and celery over chicken in baking pan.
- Combine ⅔ can milk, undiluted soup, cheese, salt and pepper.
- Pour over chicken and vegetables in pan.
- Bake for 15 minutes more at 400 degrees until sauce is bubbly and vegetables are crisp tender.
- Serves 4.

"SO LONG" TURKEY

2 tbs. butter
¼ c. flour
½ tsp. salt
¼ tsp. pepper
1 8 oz. can water chestnuts
¾ c. milk
3 c. finely chopped cooked turkey
1 egg
½ c. bread crumbs
3 tbs. butter

- Coarsely chop water chestnuts to make ½ c.
- Melt butter in a large skillet.
- Add flour, salt and pepper. Add milk. Stir until it becomes a thick sauce.
- Add chopped turkey to sauce. Cool 1-½ hours, mixed well.
- Beat egg.
- Make patties of about 2 tbs. turkey mix each. Dip in egg and then bread crumbs.
- Saute in butter about 8 minutes in a single layer in a skillet, turning to crisp and brown on both sides.
- Remove cooked patties, keeping warm in oven on an oven proof plate.
- Fry all patties, until all are done.
- Serve with hot Curry Sauce (see index) and rice.
- Makes 8 to 10 patties.

VEGETABLES

BARBECUED MIXED BEANS
CANDIED CARROTS
"CHERRY POPPER" TOMATOES
CORN FRITTERS
CORN SOUFFLE
FRIED EGGPLANT SLICES
"ESPECIALLY GOOD" BROILED TOMATOES
GYPSY HOMINY
HONEY GLAZED ONIONS
ITALIAN ZUCCHINI TOSS
NUTMEG CARROTS
PARSLEY POTATOES
POTATO STIX
RICE OR MASHED POTATO FRITTERS
SAUTEED RED BELL PEPPERS AND RED ONIONS
SAUTEED TURNIPS
SMOKEY CAULIFLOWER AU GRATIN
SWEET POTATO BALLS
SWEET RED ROSE ONIONS
TANGY RED ROSE ONIONS
YAM PANCAKES
ZUCCHINI SOUFFLE

BARBECUED MIXED BEANS

1 large red onion
2 cloves garlic
2 tbs. brown sugar
1 tsp. dry mustard
5 slices bacon
1 16 oz. can kidney beans
2 16 oz. cans Boston Baked beans
½ c. catsup or Glad's Chili Sauce (see index)
2 tbs. vinegar
¾ tsp. salt
½ tsp. pepper

- Drain kidney beans, reserving liquid. Spoon kidney and Boston Baked beans into a bowl.
- Peel and chop onion.
- Peel and mince garlic.
- Dice bacon and fry in a large skillet until crisp. Remove bacon pieces from pan, leaving 3 tbs. drippings in pan, and saving rest of drippings for other uses.
- Saute onion and garlic in bacon grease until soft, about 5 minutes.
- Stir in brown sugar, mustard, catsup or chili sauce, salt, pepper and liquid from kidney beans.
- Simmer 5 minutes. Add vinegar and bacon bits. Mix well.
- Add sauce to beans, stirring well to mix.
- Pour into a 2 qt. casserole.
- Bake, covered, 30 minutes, until well heated through and bubbly.
- Serves 6.

Cut up smoked sausage or frankfurters added to the beans makes a full meal when accompanied with a green salad and french bread.

CANDIED CARROTS

10 medium carrots
½ tsp. salt
6 tbs. brown sugar
6 tbs. butter

- Peel carrots. Cut into ½ inch wide x 3 inch long strips.
- Cook in salted boiling water until just crisp tender, about 5 minutes.
- Drain.
- Place butter and brown sugar in a large skillet and warm over low heat until well mixed.
- Drop carrots into sugar and butter mixture and saute, stirring occasionally over medium heat, until carrot strips are candied and sugar is cooked down.
- Delicious served with baked ham, pot roast, or Pork Chops Florentine (see index).
- Serves 4.

"CHERRY POPPER" TOMATOES

4 bread slices
2 doz. whole cherry tomatoes
1 small yellow onion
5 parsley sprigs
1/8 tsp. thyme
¼ tsp. salt
1/8 tsp. pepper
2 tbs. olive oil

- Wash and remove stems from tomatoes.
- Arrange in a single layer close together in a shallow baking dish.
- Peel and finely chop onion to make 2 tbs.
- Chop parsley flowerets to make 3 tbs. Discard stems.
- Break bread slices into soft bread crumbs to make ½ cup.
- Combine onion, parsley, bread crumbs, thyme, salt, pepper and olive oil.
- Sprinkle over single layer of tomatoes in pan.
- Bake, uncovered, in a 425 degree oven 6 to 8 minutes, until crumbs are toasted and tomatoes are hot, but not popped.
- These are delicious and literally pop in your mouth as you eat them!
- Serves 4.

CORN FRITTERS

¾ **c. cooked niblet corn or cream style corn**
6 tbs. Bisquick
1 egg
½ tsp. salt
¾ c. milk
½ small green pepper
6 tbs. butter

- Wash and remove membranes and seeds from pepper. Finely chop to make about 2 tbs.
- Saute green pepper in a large frying pan in 3 tbs. butter about 3 minutes.
- Add to corn in a mixing bowl.
- Add salt. Mix.
- Beat egg. Add to corn mixture. Add Bisquick and enough milk to make the right consistency of batter to fry. Beat well.
- Add the rest of the butter to the skillet and drop batter by full tablespoonsful to make 2 inch cakes.
- Fry cakes in a single layer over medium heat about 3 minutes on each side, turning once, until both sides are golden and crispy.
- Keep warm in a low oven on an oven proof plate until all are cooked.
- Makes 6 to 8 fritters.

As a starch in any meal, these fritters are tasty and quick to fix. They combine readily with almost any meat and especially well with creamed fish or chicken.

CORN SOUFFLE

1 16 oz. can cream style corn
2 tbs. flour
2 tbs. butter
3 tbs. cream
3 eggs
1 tsp. sugar
¼ tsp. salt
1/8 tsp. pepper

- Beat eggs.
- Mix flour, sugar, salt and pepper in a mixing bowl.
- Mix corn, butter cut in small pieces and cream, in another bowl.
- Add eggs to corn. Fold in the dry ingredients.
- Mix all well together.
- Pour into a buttered 1-½ qt. casserole.
- Bake, uncovered, at 350 degrees for about ¾ hour, or until a knife inserted in center comes out clean.
- Serve at once.
- Serves 4.

FRIED EGGPLANT SLICES

1 medium eggplant
1 egg
½ tsp. salt
½ c. dry bread crumbs
6 tbs. butter

- Cut off ends, peel, and slice eggplant in thin slices crosswise.
- Salt slices and sprinkle with water. Hold in a bowl until ready to fry.
- Beat egg in a shallow dish.
- Dip each slice of eggplant first in egg, carefully covering both sides, then sprinkle both sides with dry bread crumbs.
- Fry slices in butter in a single layer about 4 minutes each side until golden and crusty outside and fork tender inside. Remove slices and keep warm on an oven proof plate in a low oven, until all slices are cooked.
- Serve with Italian Meat Sauce (see index) and Mozzarella cheese sprinkled on top, or as part of Steak San Luis Obispo recipe (see index).

"ESPECIALLY GOOD" BROILED TOMATOES

6 medium to large tomatoes
½ tsp. seasoned salt
¼ tsp. pepper
¾ cube butter
¼ c. Parmesan cheese
¼ c. bread crumbs
Croutons (see index)

- Cut tomatoes crosswise in half.
- Make 3 1/8 inch deep diagonal cuts on each tomato half across center but not through.
- Press slightly to open out enough to allow the butter to melt down when broiled.
- Salt and pepper each piece.
- Place a 1/8 inch crosswise slice of cube of butter on each tomato half pressing in with finger slightly to secure.
- Sprinkle each tomato half with Parmesan cheese and dust over all with bread crumbs.
- Press croutons over top.
- Broil 4 inches from heat for 5 minutes or until butter is melted, tomato is hot and croutons are toasted and crisp.
- Serves 6.

These tomatoes may also be baked in a 350 degreee oven for 30 minutes until croutons are toasted and tomatoes are bubbly and cooked through.

GYPSY HOMINY

4 tbs. vegetable oil
2 medium carrots
1 large green pepper
2 medium zucchini, about 1 to 1-½ inches wide
4 sprigs fresh parsley
1 2 oz. jar pimento pieces, or 1 medium red bell pepper, if available.
2 medium red onions
2 14-½ oz. cans yellow or golden hominy, or 1 each of white and yellow hominy
1-¼ tsp. salt
½ tsp. pepper
2 tbs. Worcestershire sauce

- Peel and cut carrots in 3 inch long x 1/8 inch strips.
- Wash and remove membrane and seeds from green pepper, (and red pepper, if used). Cut into 3 inch long x 1/8 inch strips.
- Peel and thinly slice onions.
- Chop parsley flowerets, discarding stems, to make 4 tbs.
- Slice zucchini in thin crosswise slices.
- The vegetables may be prepared ahead of time and stored in plastic bags in the refrigerator until ready to cook.
- Drain hominy, rinsing in cold water.
- In a large skillet saute vegetables, except hominy, stir-frying in vegetable oil until crisp tender about 10 minutes. Salt to taste.
- Add hominy and Worcestershire sauce. Toss over medium heat for 5 minutes.
- Turn heat to low and cover, until ready to serve.
- Serves 6.

Great with hamburger or barbecued ribs and as an accompaniment to many Southwestern dishes.

HONEY GLAZED ONIONS

3 tbs. butter
2 tbs. honey
½ tsp. nutmeg
1 16 oz. can small white onions

- Mix butter, honey and nutmeg in a medium skillet over low heat.
- Drain onions. Remove any hard pieces of skin.
- Saute onions in honey sauce over medium heat until brown and glazed, about 10 minutes, shaking pan often to thoroughly coat onions.
- Delicious as an accompaniment to roast beef or baked ham.

ITALIAN ZUCCHINI TOSS

2 medium zucchini
3 medium White Rose potatoes
1 large yellow onion
1 clove garlic
3 tbs. olive oil
½ tsp. salt
¼ tsp. pepper
1 tbs. tomato paste
1 tsp. basil

- Peel and dice potatoes in ½ inch cubes.
- Slice zucchini crosswise in ¼ inch slices.
- Peel and thinly slice onion.
- Peel and mince garlic.
- Fry potatoes in a large skillet in olive oil until tender, about 10 minutes, turning frequently.
- Add onion, garlic, zucchini, salt and pepper. Fry, stirring until tender, about 6 minutes.
- Add tomato paste and basil. Cook 5 minutes longer.
- Serves 2.

NUTMEG CARROTS

8 to 10 medium carrots
1 c. water
3 tbs. butter
1 tbs. sugar
1 small lemon
¼ tsp. nutmeg
½ tsp. salt

- Peel and coarsely grate carrots to make 4 loosely packed cups.
- Squeeze lemon to make 1 tbs. juice.
- Cook carrots in salted boiling water until firm tender, about 5 minutes.
- Pour off water.
- Stir in butter, sugar, lemon juice and nutmeg. Mix well.
- Makes 6 servings.

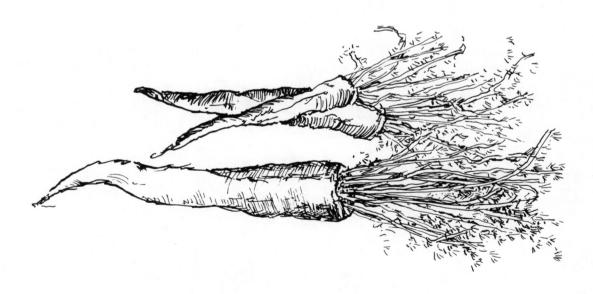

PARSLEY POTATOES

12 small red potatoes
6 parsley sprigs
1 tsp. salt
½ tsp. pepper
5 tbs. butter

- Boil potatoes in their jackets about 20 to 25 minutes until they are firm tender when pierced with a fork.
- Drain. Cool. Peel.
- Chop parsley flowerets to make 4 tbs. discarding stems.
- Melt butter in a large skillet.
- Place whole potatoes in the melted butter. Salt and pepper them and sprinkle with parsley.
- Fry 5 minutes until they are golden and crisp on the outside.
- Shake pan occasionally to cover all sides of potatoes with the parsley.
- Serves 4.

POTATO STIX

4 medium baking potatoes
¼ c. butter
1 tsp. onion salt
Paprika
¼ c. grated Parmesan cheese

- Scrub potatoes. Do not peel.
- Cut into long slices about ½ inch thick, including skins.
- Arrange in 1 layer in a large buttered baking pan.
- Melt butter. Brush potato stix with melted butter. Sprinkle with onion salt, Parmesan cheese and paprika.
- Bake in a 400 degree oven about 20 to 30 minutes until potatoes are tender and crisp, like thick "french fries".
- While baking, turn occasionally to cover with butter and cheese.

RICE OR MASHED POTATO FRITTERS

¾ c. cooked rice or cooked mashed potatoes
1 small yellow onion
2 large or 3 medium stalks of celery
6 tbs. Bisquick
1 egg
¼ tsp. salt
6 tbs. butter
5-½ oz. can evaporated milk

- Peel and finely chop onion to make about 2 tbs.
- Clean and finely chop celery to make about 3 tbs.
- Saute onion and celery in 3 tbs. butter in a large frying pan about 4 minutes.
- Add onion and celery to rice or potatoes in a mixing bowl.
- Beat egg and add to mixture in bowl. Salt to taste, stirring well.
- Add Bisquick and enough evaporated milk, about ½ can, to make a batter of the right consistency to fry the cakes. Mix well. Batter should be rather thin.
- Add rest of butter to frying pan as needed. Drop batter by full tablespoonsful into the pan in a single layer, forming fritters about 2-½ inches in diameter.
- Fry cakes over medium heat about 4 minutes each side, turning once, until golden and crisp on the outside.
- Keep fritters warm on an oven proof plate until all are cooked.
- Makes about 8 fritters.

This is a great way to use left over rice or mashed potatoes. Left over mashed sweet potato fritters are delicious accompaniments to fried ham or pork chops.

SAUTEED RED BELL PEPPERS AND RED ONIONS

4 medium red onions
4 large red Bell peppers
2 cloves garlic
2 tbs. vegetable oil
2 tbs. butter
2 tbs. crushed basil leaves

- Peel and thinly slice onions.
- Remove membranes and seed from red peppers. Slice into thin strips.
- Peel and mince garlic.
- Saute garlic and onions in a large frying pan in oil and butter until onions are limp and golden, about 8 minutes. Add pepper strips.
- Cook 10 minutes more over moderate heat, stirring to prevent sticking.
- Stir in basil.
- Add more butter if necesary. Serve hot.
- Serves 6 to 8.

SAUTEED TURNIPS

8 medium turnips
6 slices bacon
1 large yellow onion
½ c. chicken broth
1 tsp. sugar
½ tsp. salt
3 sprigs parsley
1 small lemon
¼ tsp. pepper

- Squeeze lemon to make about 1 tbs.
- Chop flowerets of parsley, discarding stems, to make 2 tbs.
- Peel and cut turnips into ¼ inch cubes to make about 3 cupsful.
- Peel and chop onion.
- Dice bacon. Fry until crisp. Remove bacon pieces from pan, discarding all but 2 tbs. grease. (Save rest of drippings for other uses.)
- Saute onion in bacon drippings about 5 minutes, until golden.
- Add turnips, chicken broth, sugar and salt to onions in pan.
- Cook, covered, stirring occasionally, for 5 minutes, until tender.
- Uncover and saute, shaking pan, until all liquid is evaporated.
- Add bacon pieces, parsley, lemon juice and pepper. Toss.
- Serve at once.
- Serves 4.

SMOKEY CAULIFLOWER AU GRATIN

1 large fresh cauliflower
2 tbs. butter
1 c. water
1 medium green pepper
2 tbs. flour
¼ tsp. pepper
½ tsp. salt
¾ cup milk
¼ lb. sharp Cheddar cheese
½ tsp. Worcestershire sauce
½ lb. piece beef smoked sausage
1 c. buttered croutons (see index)

- Remove membranes and seeds from green pepper and chop to make ¼ cup.
- Coarsely shred cheese.
- Clean and remove leaves from cauliflower. Cut flowerets into large bite size pieces.
- Cook in boiling water only until just firm tender, about 5 minutes. Drain.
- Place pieces of cauliflower in a buttered baking dish.
- Remove casing from sausage and thinly slice crosswise. Spread over cauliflower in casserole.
- Saute green pepper in butter until tender soft, about 5 minutes.
- Add flour, salt and pepper. Pour in milk. Cook, stirring. Add shredded cheese and Worcestershire sauce. Cook until cheese is melted and sauce is creamy.
- Pour cheese sauce over contents of casserole. Top with croutons.
- Bake at 400 degrees for 25 minutes uncovered.

SWEET POTATO BALLS

1 16 oz. can yams
1 15 oz. can pineapple chunks
4 tbs. melted butter
¼ tsp. salt
¼ c. cracker crumbs
½ tsp. ground nutmeg
1 tbs. brown sugar

- Drain and mash yams in a mixing bowl.
- Add melted butter, brown sugar, salt and nutmeg. Mix well.
- Drain pineapple chunks, reserving liquid for other uses.
- By hand, shape enough potato around each chunk of pineapple to cover, making balls about the size of a golf ball.
- Roll balls gently in cracker crumbs.
- Pour rest of melted butter in a shallow baking pan. Place sweet potato balls in pan about 1 inch apart.
- Bake in a 350 degree oven about 15 minutes, or until balls are golden brown, turning once or twice to brown all sides.
- Serve hot with ham or turkey.
- Makes 20 to 24 balls.

SWEET RED ROSE ONIONS

4 large red onions
½ tsp. salt
¾ cube butter
¼ c. honey
¼ c. brown sugar
3 tsp. ground nutmeg

- Peel onions and slice ½ inch off top.
- Cut onions diagonally 4 times each through center downward, but not through. Open up like a half blown rose.
- Place each onion in a 10 inch square of aluminum foil, enough to amply enclose the onion.
- Salt each onion to taste.
- Soften butter and mix with sugar and honey.
- Spoon butter mixture, about 3 to 4 tsp., over each onion, forcing down into cuts where possible.
- Sprinkle with nutmeg.
- Wrap securely with foil, folding over top in a seam and tucking up ends.
- Place in a baking pan. Bake in a 400 degree oven for 45 minutes.
- These may be barbecued, placing them in their foil jackets around the edges of the grill while barbecuing, for about 60 minutes.
- Serve in foil rolled down around the onions to preserve the juices.
- Great with beef, pork or ham.
- Serves 4.

TANGY RED ROSE ONIONS

4 large red onions
Hickory smoke salt
½ c. butter
¼ c. crumbled roquefort or blue cheese
8 drops liquid hot sauce

- Peel onions. Slice off ½ inch from the top.
- Cut onions diagonally 4 times each through center downward, but not through. Open up like a half blown rose.
- Place each onion in a 10 inch square of aluminum foil, enough to amply enclose the onion.
- Sprinkle with hickory smoke salt to taste.
- Mix softened butter and cheese together. Add hot sauce and mix well.
- Spoon about 2 to 3 tsp. cheese mixture in each onion, forcing down in cuts as much as possible.
- Wrap securely with foil, folding over top in a seam and tucking up ends.
- Place in a baking pan. Bake in a 400 degree oven for 45 minutes.
- These may be barbecued, placing them in their foil jackets around the edges of the hot grill while barbecuing, for about 60 minutes.
- Serve in foil rolled down around the onions to preserve the juices.
- Great with chicken or fish.
- Serves 4.

YAM PANCAKES

2 eggs
1 1 lb.-13 oz. can sweet potatoes or yams
2 stalks celery
1 medium yellow onion
¼ c. Bisquick
1 tsp. ground nutmeg
1 tsp. curry powder
1 tsp. salt
¼ tsp. cayenne pepper
¾ cube butter

- Drain and mash sweet potatoes. Place in a mixing bowl.
- Peel and grate onion. Squeeze out juice.
- Chop celery.
- Beat egg.
- Add egg, onion and celery to mashed potatoes.
- Add Bisquick, nutmeg, curry, salt and pepper. Mix well.
- Melt 3 tbs. butter in a large skillet over medium heat.
- Add tablespoonsful of potato mixture to form pancakes.
- Cook in butter until brown. Turn to cook other side until golden, about 4 minutes each side.
- Remove cakes as done to oven proof plate in low oven to keep warm until all are cooked, adding more butter as necessary to skillet.
- Especially good served with ham, turkey, or chicken.
- Makes 12 to 14 pancakes.

ZUCCHINI SOUFFLE

7 or 8 medium zucchini
5 slices stale bread
3 tbs. butter
¼ tsp. seasoned salt
4 eggs
1 large yellow onion
3 tbs. butter
¼ c. Parmesan cheese

- Cut ends off zucchini and slice in ¼ inch slices to make 6 cups.
- Peel and chop onion.
- Fry zucchini and onion in butter in a large skillet until tender, about 10 minutes, salting to taste.
- Break up bread slices to make 1-½ cups soft stale bread crumbs.
- Add zucchini and onion to bread crumbs in a large mixing bowl combining well.
- Separate eggs.
- Beat yolks and add to zucchini mixture.
- Beat egg whites until stiff and fold into zucchini mixture.
- Pour into a 2 qt. buttered casserole. Sprinkle with grated Parmesan cheese.
- Bake, uncovered, for 30 minutes at 350 degrees until eggs are set.
- Serve at once.
- Delicious with creamed shrimp or tuna.
- Serves 6.

FISH

AVOCADO FILLED WITH CURRIED SHRIMP
AVOCADO WITH PARSLEY AND SHRIMP SAUCE
BAKED HALIBUT SLICES
CLAM OR CRAB FRITTERS
CRAB STUFFED BELL PEPPERS
HANGTOWN FRY
NO-FAIL SHRIMP SOUFFLE
OVERNIGHT SALMON CASSEROLE
SALMON CAKES
SWISS CHEESE PIE WITH CRAB MEAT SAUCE
SALMON QUICHE
TROUT FILLETS

AVOCADO FILLED WITH CURRIED SHRIMP

1 lb. fresh or frozen medium cooked shrimp
1 tbs. butter
1-½ tsp. curry powder, or to taste
1 tsp. salt
1 medium tomato
1 medium yellow onion
1 large lemon
1 c. sour cream
3 or 4 large avocados

- Defrost shrimp, if frozen. Squeeze lemon to make about 2 tbs.
- Peel and chop tomato and onion.
- Melt butter in a large skillet, stirring with curry powder and salt.
- Add the chopped vegetables.
- Cook gently until vegetables are soft, about 5 minutes.
- Add lemon juice and shrimp.
- Add sour cream slowly, stirring.
- Heat mixture before serving.
- Halve and peel avocados. Discard seeds.
- Place each half on a plate. Fill center to overflowing with hot curried shrimp mixture. Serve with buttered rice.
- Serves 6 or 8.

This also may be served by dicing the avocados and adding directly to curried shrimp before serving. Spoon the warmed mixture over the rice. Not quite as spectacular as the filled half of avocado, but just as good.

AVOCADO WITH PARSLEY AND SHRIMP SAUCE

4 oz. cream cheese
2 tbs. butter
1 clove garlic
½ c. cream
¼ lb. cooked shrimp
1 medium lemon
¼ tsp. salt
Dash of pepper
4 sprigs of parsley
2 medium avocados

- Wash parsley, discard stems and chop flowerets to make about ¼ cup.
- Peel and mince garlic. Squeeze lemon to make 1-½ tsp. juice.
- Melt butter and cream cheese in a large skillet. Add garlic. Stir and blend.
- Add cream and heat. Do not boil.
- Add shrimp, lemon juice, salt and pepper. Blend gently.
- Peel, seed and halve avocados.
- Pour shrimp sauce over halves and serve hot with rice.
- Serves 4 for luncheon, or a light supper.

BAKED HALIBUT SLICES

4 ½ inch thick slices halibut
2 tbs. butter
1 medium lemon
1 medium yellow onion
Paprika
3 tbs. butter
½ c. Half and Half cream
¼ c. Sauterne wine
½ tsp. thyme
½ tsp. salt
¼ tsp. pepper
3 sprigs parsley
3 tbs. grated Parmesan cheese

- Butter a shallow baking dish large enough to hold fish slices in 1 layer.
- Rub halibut slices with lemon juice. Place fish in baking dish.
- Peel and chop onion. Spread over fish. Dot with butter.
- Sprinkle with paprika.
- Mix cream, Sauterne, thyme, salt and pepper. Pour over fish in baking dish.
- Chop parsley flowerets, discarding stems. Sprinkle over fish.
- Sprinkle Parmesan cheese over all.
- Bake, uncovered, 25 to 30 minutes, until fish is flaky but not dry and separates easily when pulled with a fork.
- Other similar slices of fish may be prepared in this manner also.

CLAM OR CRAB FRITTERS

FOR THE FRITTER BATTER

1 6-½ oz. can minced clams, or 1 6 oz. can crab meat
1 medium stalk celery
1 small yellow onion
4 tbs. butter
6 tbs. Bisquick
1 egg
½ tsp. garlic salt
¼ tsp. pepper
¾ c. milk
1 tsp. dried leaf thyme

FOR SPECIAL SAUCE

½ c. mayonnaise
2 tbs. Sherry wine
Dash hot sauce

TO MAKE FRITTERS

- Drain all but about 2 tbs. juice from clams, or clean crab meat, removing any bones and cartilage.
- Finely chop celery to make 2 tbs.
- Peel and finely chop onion to make 2 tbs.
- Beat egg.
- Saute celery and onion in 2 tbs. butter 3 minutes. Add garlic salt, thyme and pepper.
- Mix with clams or crab in a bowl. Add egg. Mix.
- Add Bisquick and enough milk to make the right consistency of batter for frying into fritters.
- Add rest of butter to skillet.
- Drop batter by full tbs. into pan. Fry fritters in a single layer over medium heat about 3 minutes each side until browned and crispy and cooked through. Add more butter if needed to prevent sticking to pan. Keep fritters warm until all are cooked.
- Makes 6 to 8 fritters. Serve hot with special sauce.

TO MAKE SPECIAL SAUCE

Mix mayonnaise, a dash of hot sauce and enough Sherry to thin to desired consistency, about 3 tbs. Serve as an accompaniment for fish fritters.

213

CRAB STUFFED BELL PEPPERS

4 medium Bell peppers
3 c. water
½ tsp. salt
1 medium yellow onion
2 large or 3 medium stalks of celery
2 slices bacon
½ c. bread crumbs
2 tbs. butter
1-½ c. fresh crab meat, or 2 6 oz. cans crab
2 eggs
2 tbs.dry Sherry
Paprika

- Cut peppers in half lengthwise. Remove membranes and seeds. Place in salted boiling water.
- Cook until crisp tender, about 5 minutes. Remove to drain on paper towels.
- Peel and dice onion. Dice celery. Cut bacon into small pieces.
- In a medium skillet over medium heat, saute bacon, onion and celery until vegetables are crisp, about 5 minutes.
- Flake crab meat, removing all cartilage and shell bits.
- Slightly beat eggs. Add Sherry and crab meat. Add bread crumbs.
- Mix well and add to vegetables and bacon in skillet. Stir.
- Fill pepper halves. Arrange in a shallow baking pan. Sprinkle with paprika.
- Bake in a 350 degree oven, 20 minutes, until hot.
- Sprightly sauce (see index) may be served as an accompaniment.
- If you prefer a milder sauce, use a regular cream sauce brightened with ½ c. shredded mild Cheddar cheese.
- Or just serve with a quarter of a lemon to squeeze on top.

GLADYS WORDEN CRUM '87

Fast Delivery From San Francisco
To "Hangtown" Placerville, California
Eighteen Hundred And Forty Nine

HANGTOWN FRY

Placerville, California, on the Forty Nine Highway, route of the California gold rush in eighteen hundred and forty nine, was originally called "Hangtown". We read that it was a wild and jumping town where justice (?) was administered quickly by hanging the culprit (?) to the nearest stalwart oak tree. Be that as it may, these miners were fortunately overweighted with gold nuggets in their pockets and sought to expand their renown by showing their wealth through any spectacular method available. Sometimes they went to great imaginative lengths to prove their point.

One enterprising fellow, bound to out-do his buddies, sent for fresh oysters, packed in ice, to be galloped on horseback post haste over the dirt roads of the day, from San Francisco all the way to Hangtown. He had them served for breakfast, which further astonished everyone. They are still served there, in the foothills of the Sierras and far and wide are known as "Hangtown Fry".

There are several versions, but I find this recipe very adequate and satisfying. We serve it today as a light supper.

> **6 eggs**
> **½ c. ale or beer**
> **½ tsp. salt**
> **Dash of liquid hot sauce to taste**
> **12 medium oysters, shucked and cleaned or 1 pint fresh oysters**
> **6 bacon slices**

- Drain oysters well, and cut into bite size pieces if too large.
- Beat eggs thoroughly with beer, salt and hot sauce.
- Dice bacon and fry in a large skillet until almost crisp. Remove all but 2 tbs. of bacon grease and fry oysters until half the juices are evaporated and edges begin to curl, about 5 minutes.
- Pour off rest of juice.
- Over medium heat, pour egg mixture over oysters in pan. Cook and stir until eggs are scrambled.
- Serves 2 generously.
- Serve with sourdough bread toast.

NO-FAIL SHRIMP SOUFFLE

4 eggs
1-½ c. milk
½ tsp. salt
¼ tsp. pepper
1 8 oz. can sliced water chestnuts
1 lb. small cooked shrimp
½ lb. sharp Cheddar cheese
8 slices fresh white bread
1 tsp. dry mustard
4 or 5 green onions
½ cube butter
½ tsp. paprika

- Cut crusts off bread slices and cut into 1 inch cubes.
- Coarsely grate cheese, or cut into 1 inch squares, if sliced, to make about ¾ cup.
- Peel and thinly slice green onions, to make 4 tbs., including 2 inches of stems.
- Drain water chestnuts.
- Beat eggs, mustard, milk, salt and pepper together.
- Cover bottom of a 2-½ qt. greased casserole with a layer of bread cubes.
- Spread half the onions, half the water chestnuts, half the shrimp and half the cheese over the layer of bread cubes.
- Put another layer of bread cubes over the shrimp layer.
- Repeat the process, ending with a third layer of bread cubes as the topping.
- Pour milk and egg mixture over the filled casserole.
- Dot with butter and sprinkle with paprika.
- Cover an refrigerate overnight.
- Bake uncovered at 350 degrees for ¾ to 1 hour, until bubbly and top bread pieces are toasted.
- This may also be made with crab.
- Serves 6.

OVERNIGHT SALMON CASSEROLE

1 7-¼ oz. can salmon, or 1 cup fresh baked salmon
6 slices white bread
½ c. mayonnaise
4 eggs
2 medium yellow or white onions
1 8 oz. can water chestnuts
1 medium green pepper
2 c. milk
1 11 oz. can cream of mushroom soup
¼ lb. sharp Cheddar cheese

- Drain and flake salmon, reserving liquid. Discard skin and bones.
- Cut bread slices in cubes to make about 4 cups.
- Place ½ of the bread cubes in a 2-½ qt. casserole.
- Peel and chop onions to make ¾ cup.
- Drain and coarsely chop water chestnuts.
- Remove membranes and seeds and coarsely chop green pepper to make ¾ cup.
- Mix salmon, onions, water chestnuts, green pepper and mayonnaise together.
- Spread over bread cubes in casserole and top with rest of bread cubes.
- Beat eggs. Mix with milk, salmon liquid and undiluted soup.
- Pour over contents in casserole. Cover. Refrigerate overnight.
- Grate cheese. Top casserole with cheese to taste when ready to bake.
- Bake at 350 degrees for 1 hour and 15 minutes, until top is melted and golden and salmon is bubbly.
- Serves 6.

Hint: When baking a whole piece of salmon, measure fish at thickest part and allow 10 minutes baking time for each inch of thickness. Bake in a hot oven at 425 degrees. Fish should flake. Do not overbake.

SALMON CAKES

1 16 oz. can salmon
3 tbs. butter
1 medium yellow onion
3 stalks celery
1 egg
¼ c. mayonnaise
1 medium lemon
2 tsp. crushed dill weed
½ tsp. celery salt
¼ tsp. pepper
5 fresh bread slices
¼ c. flour

- Squeeze lemon to make 1 tbs. juice.
- Drain and flake salmon, removing skin and bones. Place meat in a bowl.
- Peel and finely chop onion to make about ½ cup. Chop celery to make ⅓ c.
- Lightly beat egg.
- Remove crusts from bread slices and break slices into small bits.
- Saute onion and celery in a medium skillet in 1-½ tbs. butter for 5 minutes.
- Add lemon juice, dill, celery salt and pepper. Stir. Cool.
- Add egg, bread crumbs and mayonnaise.
- Add sauteed vegetables, blending well into the salmon mixture.
- Shape into 2-½ inch flat cakes. Cover and refrigerate until ready to cook.
- The cakes may be frozen at this stage.
- After defrosting, sprinkle both sides of each cake with flour.
- Fry in 1-½ tbs. butter in a single layer over medium heat, about 5 minutes on each side until golden brown and crispy on outside. Add more butter to pan if needed. Keep cakes warm in oven on oven proof plate, until all are done.
- Makes 6 to 8 cakes.

These fish cakes are delicious served with curried cream sauce (see index), creamed shrimp sauce, or just by themselves with Tartar sauce and fresh lemon quarters.

SWISS CHEESE PIE WITH CRAB MEAT SAUCE

1 unbaked 9 inch Flaky Pie Crust shell (see index)
4 eggs
1-½ c. light cream
½ tsp. salt
1/8 tsp. ground nutmeg
½ lb. Swiss cheese
1 6 oz. can crab meat, or ¼ lb. fresh crab meat
2 tbs. butter
2 tsp. flour
1/8 tsp. salt
1 c. cream

- Bake pastry shell at 450 degrees for 7 minutes. Remove from oven.
- Reduce oven temperature to 350 degrees.
- Grate cheese to make about 1-½ cups.
- Separate eggs. Beat yolks.
- Combine yolks with cream and nutmeg.
- Beat egg whites. Fold into yolk mixture. Fold in grated cheese.
- Pour into partially baked pie shell.
- Bake at 350 degrees 40 to 45 minutes until a knife thrust in center comes out clean. Remove from oven and let stand on a wire rack 5 minutes before serving.
- To make sauce, flake crab meat, removing any bones or cartilage. Heat in butter in a medium pan.
- Blend in flour and salt, stirring. Add cream, stir until thickened.
- Serve hot over a warm slice of cheese pie.

SALMON QUICHE

1 7-½ oz. can salmon
4 green onions
2 tbs. butter
½ tsp. dill weed
1 unbaked Flaky Pie Crust Shell (see index)
1 c. shredded Swiss cheese
3 eggs
½ tsp. salt
¼ tsp. pepper
1 c. half-and-half cream
½ tsp. dry mustard

- Peel and thinly slice lower 3 inches of each onion, including part of the stem. Saute in a large skillet in butter until limp, but still bright green, about 3 minutes.
- Flake salmon, removing all bones and skin. Mix salmon and dill weed into the sauteed onions. Place mixture in unbaked pastry shell.
- Shred Swiss cheese to make 1 cup, sprinkling over salmon in pastry shell.
- Beat eggs with half-and-half, salt, pepper and mustard. Pour over cheese and salmon.
- Bake uncovered about 10 minutes at 450 degrees. Reduce heat to 350 degrees and bake for 20 to 25 minutes longer, until knife inserted in center comes out clean. Remove from oven.
- Place on a wire rack and let stand 3 minutes before cutting to serve.

***Fishing For Trout
In A Mountain Stream***

TROUT FILLETS

Did you ever taste "just-caught" trout cooked in bacon grease over a camp-fire? There is nothing quite like it. Almost as tantilizing is the way our son cooks his freshly caught trout in the old Victorian kitchen of his home in Boulder, Colorado. If the fish are large enough, the ultimate treat is a serving of trout fillets. However, the fish are delicious just cleaned and fried whole. In fact, any good white fish fillet is delicious cooked this way.

4 trout, cleaned and ready to cook, or 8 fillets
1 tsp. Worcestershire sauce
1 tsp. salt
¼ c. flour
¼ c. vegetable oil
5 tbs. butter
1 large yellow onion
2 tsp. parsley flakes
½ tsp. dried tarragon

- Peel and finely chop onion.
- Squeeze lemon to make 3 tbs. juice.
- Sprinkle each side of fillets with 4 or 5 drops Worcestershire sauce.
- Salt fish lightly.
- Sprinkle both sides of fillets with flour.
- In a large iron skillet, over high heat, fry the fish in hot oil about 2 to 3 minutes each side. They will be crisp on the outside and tender flaky inside.
- Remove to an oven proof plate and keep warm in a low oven.
- Pour off oil from skillet. Add butter to skillet.
- Stir in onion, lemon juice, chopped parsley and tarragon. Heat and stir until butter is melted and onion is golden. Pour over fillets.
- Serves 4.

SOUTHWESTERN SPECIALTIES

CARMELITA HUEVOS RANCHEROS
CARMELITA HUEVOS RANCHEROS SAUCE
BASIC ALL PURPOSE BEANS
BLACK BEAN CHILI
CALIFORNIA CAMPFIRE CHILI
CHILI MEAT LOAF
EASY FIXIN' MEXICAN CHICKEN THIGHS
CORN CHIP TACOS (SOMBREROS)
CHIMICHANGAS
CRAB ENCHILADAS (SAN FRANCISCO SPECIAL)
CREAM STYLE CHICKEN ENCHILADAS
FIESTA CHICKEN
FRESH SALSA
GUACAMOLE SPEARS
INDISPENSABLE GUACAMOLE
LIVER AND ONION OLE
MEXICAN POT ROAST
NOGALES SALAD
OVEN CHILE RELLENOS
QUESO CALIENTE DIP
REFRIED BEANS
SOUTHWESTERN CHEESE ENCHILADAS
TOSTADA DE POLLO (CHICKEN TOSTADAS)

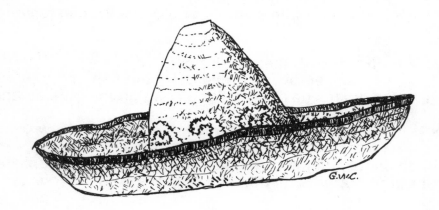

SOME LIKE IT HOT!

COOKING WITH THE
SOUTHWESTERN TOUCH

All of us may not live with a string of dried chiles hanging on our kitchen wall and a pot of beans and chili forever simmering on the back of the stove, as is the custom in the southwestern states of the United States. But, we have been exposed to the typical cooking of this area with its Mexican influence, through more commercial channels. The spices and electric flavors of Mexican cooking have gradually seeped northward and eastward over the United States until scarcely anyone has not now experienced the delight of "south of the border" cooking at some time or another. In California, serving chili and beans and tacos is indeed a part of our way of life.

Here are just a handful of my favorite recipes with that southwestern zing. I do not profess to be an expert in preparing Mexican dishes, but I know and enjoy those presented here, using canned Mexican products now available, such as green chiles, hot sauce and "store bought" tortillas. We have all found simple versions colorful and tasty. The chile flavor may be altered to suit the individual palates.

ABOUT CHILI

To those who love the deep zest of chili, it is an exciting dish, rousing the senses and warming the heart. Basically, chili is any kind of meat or combination of meats cooked with chile peppers, spices and certain other ingredients. It is the personality of the creative cook that gives it that surprising flair.

We are told that its origins lie with the cowboy chuck wagon cooks of the southwest in the cowboy stew they served as regular fare. Each cook had his own special concoction involving spices, meat and chile, tempered or enchanced by availability of supplies and the imagination of the cook.

It is the same today. Some cooks prefer serving their chili in a bowl, unadulterated by the addition of beans. Others add the beans to thicken the sauce. Served with a salad, or salsa, it is an universal meal in the area where it originated, southwest Texas and Mexico. Now it is embraced in the United States as part of American fare and has taken its place along with hamburgers and hot dogs.

We are told that English settlers in Texas invented chile powder as a convenient way of making Mexican type dishes in eighteen hundred thirty five.

Hint: "Chile" — the vegetable.
"Chili — the concoction.

"Los Tres Panchos"

CARMELITA HUEVOS RANCHEROS

There are many versions of this fun breakfast. This one I can remember particularly because it was served to us one sunny morning at a patio table in Carmel, California, which is quite "a ways" from Mexico. Yet it seemed delightfully appropriate, with the salty air of the Pacific ocean as an accompaniment. Perhaps because Monterey, only a few miles away, was an original Mexican colony? Vive el desayuno!

2 large flour tortillas
1 c. Huevos Rancheros sauce (see index)
1 tbs. chile powder
¼ lb. sharp Cheddar cheese
8 link pork sausages
4 eggs
1 c. guacamole (see index)
12 corn chips
1 c. refried beans (see index)

- Grate cheese to make about 6 tbs.
- Fry pork sausages until browned. Remove from pan, drain on paper towels, and keep warm on an oven proof plate in a low oven.
- Wrap tortillas loosely but securely in aluminum foil. Warm in low oven for 15 minutes. Warm Rancheros sauce.
- Cook eggs soft boiled, or if you prefer, fry them sunny side up.
- Place tortillas on 2 large warmed serving plates.
- Pour ¼ c. Rancheros sauce on each warm tortilla.
- Have the beans warm, mixed with chile powder and cheese melted in them.
- Place 2 eggs in center of each tortilla, 2 pork sausages on each end.
- Arrange guacamole on one side and beans on the other.
- Tuck 3 corn chips in beans and 3 in guacamole.
- Pour rest of warm Ranchero sauce over all.
- Serve at once.
- Serves 2.

A beautiful bounteous brunch, Southwestern style!

CARMELITA HUEVOS RANCHEROS SAUCE

1 12 oz. jar picante sauce
½ c. Glad's Chili sauce (see index) or any commerical
   cocktail chili sauce
1 large tomato
2 medium stalks celery
1 large avocado

- Chop celery fine.
- Peel and chop tomato.
- Peel avocado, discarding seed. Coarsely chop avocado.
- Add celery, tomato, avocado and chili sauce to picante sauce in a
  medium cooking pan.
- Mix gently to heat and serve.
- Best to use over Carmelita Huevos Rancheros (see index) or
  Tostados de Pollo (see index).

GLADYS WORDEN CRUM '87

BASIC ALL PURPOSE BEANS

1 lb. pinto beans
1 large yellow onion
4 slices thick bacon
3 tsp. chile powder
1 tsp. salt

- Peel and chop onion.
- Dice bacon.
- Wash beans. Cover with water and soak overnight.
- When ready to cook beans the next day, drain soaked beans and add fresh water to cover, plus 1 inch.
- Add onion and diced bacon and simmer at least 2 hours, adding more water if they become too dry. Stir occasionally to prevent sticking.
- When beans are tender, add salt and chile powder to taste. Cook 20 minutes more.
- This makes about 5 cups of basic beans.

BLACK BEAN CHILI

**1 lb. black beans, (obtainable at Mexican Food Stores), or
   pinto beans
2 tsp. salt
6 to 8 c. water
3 lbs. ½ inch thick round steak
2 tbs. bacon grease
3 tbs. peanut oil
3 large yellow or red onions
2 large green peppers
2 cloves garlic
2 4 oz. cans whole green chiles
4 tbs. chile powder, or to taste
2-½ tsp. cumin
2 bay leaves
Salt and pepper to taste
3 c. beef bouillon
2 26 oz. cans tomatoes
1 6 oz. can tomato paste**

- Clean and rinse beans. Cover with water to 1 inch above beans.
- Let stand overnight.
- Drain and add about 6 c. clear water to the soaked beans. Add salt.
- Bring to a boil in a large kettle and simmer for 1 hour or until just tender.
- Drain, retaining about 1 cup of the juice. Set cooked beans aside in a bowl.
- Cut round steak into ½ inch cubes.
- Saute meat in bacon grease until gray, in a large skillet.
- Remove with a slotted spoon to another bowl.
- Remove membranes and seeds of peppers and chop to make approximately 1-½ cups.
- Peel and chop onions to make about 1-½ cups.
- Peel and chop garlic. Drain and remove seeds from canned chiles.
- Add peanut oil to the large kettle. Add vegetables and cook, stirring, for 5 minutes.
- Add beef broth, tomatoes and tomato paste, stirring occasionally to prevent burning, for 2-½ hours until thick. Break apart any big pieces of meat with a spoon.
- Add beans with their juice. Simmer 15 minutes.
- Discard bay leaves. If necessary to thin out, add water or more beef bouillon.
- Chili should be thick.
- Taste for flavors, adding more chile or salt if needed.
- Serves 6 to 8.

CALIFORNIA CAMPFIRE CHILI

This is straight chili. It may be made with left over pot roast of beef, well done and tender enough to shred easily. Or start with 4 lbs. of beef stew meat. At any rate, well done shredded beef is the basis.

4 lbs. beef stew meat
2 tbs. bacon grease
1 15 oz. can tomato sauce
1 c. Glad's Chili Sauce (see index), or a commercial chili sauce will do
1 c. water
1 can beef bouillon
4 or 5 tbs. chile powder, or to taste
1 tbs. oregano
1 tsp. cumin
1 large red or yellow onion
2 cloves garlic
1 tsp. salt
2 tsp. sugar
1 tsp. paprika
2 heaping tsp. flour
3 tsp. water

- Cook meat in a large deep pot roast kettle in bacon grease over high heat until well browned. Add bouillon, undiluted, and simmer until tender, about 1-½ hours. Add more water if necessary to prevent meat from sticking to pan. When very tender, shred with a fork in the kettle. (If using left over pot roast, shred and add bouillon with water and tomato sauce.)
- Peel and chop onion.
- Peel and mince garlic.
- Add onion and garlic to tomato sauce and meat in the kettle.
- Cook and simmer 15 minutes.
- Add chile powder, oregano, cumin, salt and pepper. Add paprika.
- Stir and simmer at least another hour until thick, adding more water or bouillon if needed.
- The longer it cooks, the better it is. Adjust flavors to suit individual tastes.
- When ready to serve, thicken with flour mixed with water, if desired.
- Serves 6 to 8, either alone with bread or crackers, or as a thick sauce over tamales, rice, or warmed slices of Chile Meat Loaf (see index).

As an added adventure, use left over "Honey-Do" Steak (see index), shredded or cut into slivers, as a basis for a sweeter California Campfire Chili.

CHILI MEAT LOAF

1 c. Glad's Chili sauce, or any commercial cocktail chili sauce
3 tbs. chile powder
1 tsp. salt
1 4 oz. can diced green chiles
1-½ lbs. ground beef
1 egg
1 c. soft bread crumbs
1 c. basic Mexican beans (see index)
¾ lb. sharp Cheddar cheese
1 tbs. chile powder
½ tsp. salt
3 tbs. water

- Beat egg.
- Combine ground beef, salt, egg, bread crumbs and half the chili sauce, half the diced chiles and 3 tbs. chile powder.
- Mix well.
- Shape ¾ of the meat mixture into a loaf. Place in a shallow baking pan.
- Press a large center cavity in the loaf.
- Grate cheese to make about 1 cup.
- Mash beans, adding cheese, 1 tbs. chile powder and half the remaining chili sauce. Mix well and spoon into the cavity of the meat loaf.
- Spread last of the meat mixture over the bean filling, pinching and shaping into rest of the loaf to completely seal the loaf.
- Spread last of the chili sauce evenly over the top.
- Pour a little water, about 3 tbs., around loaf in pan. Bake at 375 degrees for 1 hour.
- Slice to serve.

Hint: "Chile" — the vegetable.
       "Chili" — the concoction.

"EASY FIXIN" MEXICAN CHICKEN THIGHS

1 1.2 oz. pkg. chili seasoning mix
8 chicken thighs
3 tbs. vegetable oil
3 c. cookied Basic Mexican beans (see index), or 2 16-½
   oz. cans kidney beans
1 c. water

- Fry chicken thighs in oil about 10 minutes in a large skillet, turning to brown both sides.
- If using cooked Mexican beans, set aside ¾ c. water.
- If using canned kidney beans, drain, reserving liquid.
- Place beans in a 2 qt. casserole.
- Place browned chicken thighs on top of beans.
- Blend water, chili mix and liquid from canned beans or ¾ c. water.
- Pour blended mixture over chicken and beans in casserole.
- Bake covered, in a 350 degree oven, for 50 minutes until hot and bubbly and chicken is tender.
- May be frozen.
- Serves 4.

CORN CHIP TACOS
(SOMBREROS)

1 tsp. salt
2 tsp. chile powder, or to taste
1 lb. ground chuck
4 stalks celery
1 small green pepper
1 medium yellow onion
2 tbs. butter
1 10 oz. can tomatoes
Corn chips
¼ lb. Jack cheese
Lettuce
Guacamole (see index)

- Sprinkle salt, chile powder over ground chuck. Let stand 1 hour.
- Remove membranes and seeds from green pepper. Chop to make about ¼ cup.
- Chop celery fine to make about ½ cup.
- Shred cheese to make 1 cup.
- Shred lettuce to make 1 cup.
- Cook celery, green pepper and onion in butter in a large frying pan, 8 minutes, stirring, until vegetables are firm tender.
- Add meat. Fry until meat is brown and most of the juice is evaporated. Stir often.
- Add tomatoes and tomato sauce.
- Simmer 30 minutes until thick.
- To serve, place a handful of corn chips on a serving plate. Spoon meat sauce over them and sprinkle with lettuce and cheese. A spoonful of Guacamole on top of each serving is an added bonus.

CHIMICHANGAS

3 c. well done beef pot roast, shredded
12 10 inch flour tortillas
3 tbs. chile powder
2 tsp. oregano
1 tsp. ground cumin
1 tsp. garlic salt
½ c. olive oil
2 tbs. vinegar
1-½ c. water
Head of lettuce
2 c. guacamole (see index)

- Place shredded tender beef in a deep cooking pot.
- Sprinkle with chile powder, oregano, cumin and salt.
- Mix vinegar and water and pour over meat. Mix. Bring to a boil and simmer about ½ hour until water is almost evaporated and mixture is thick.
- Stir occasionally watching closely so as not to burn meat.
- Wrap stacked tortillas in aluminum foil. Heat in a 350 degree oven for 15 minutes. Spoon ½ c. meat mixture on each tortilla. Fold over sides and one end of tortilla. Roll up. Fasten with wooden picks if needed.
- Fry Chimichangas in ½ inch hot oil in a large skillet 1 minute on each side until golden brown.
- Remove with tongs and drain on paper towels. Keep warm on an oven proof plate in a low oven until all are done.
- Serve garnished with shredded lettuce and guacamole.
- You may serve salsa (see index) on the side, for an added treat.
- Serves 6.

CRAB ENCHILADAS
(SAN FRANCISCO SPECIAL)

1 c. salsa (see index)
6 corn tortillas
¼ c. vegetable oil
1-½ c. fresh crab meat or 3 6 oz. cans crab meat
12 crab leg meat sections (if available)
3 tbs. butter
2 medium yellow onions
½ lb. Jack cheese
¼ c. pitted black olives
¾ c. sour cream

- Peel and chop onions to make 6 tbs.
- Grate cheese to make 1-½ cups.
- Peel, seed and slice avocado into long ¼ inch slices.
- Peel and thinly slice tomatoes.
- Remove bones and cartilage from crab meat and flake.
- Heat oil in large skillet. Dip tortillas in hot oil for 20 seconds, only until soft. Remove with tongs.
- Place ¼ c. crab meat in center of each tortilla.
- Add 1 tbs. chopped onion and 1 tbs. salsa to each crab filled tortilla.
- Roll and place close together, seam side down in a baking pan.
- Cover with remaining salsa and sprinkle with cheese.
- Bake at 400 degrees for 10 minutes until hot and bubbly.
- Serve with a dollop of sour cream on each. Garnish with 3 or 4 olives, tomato slices and crab legs (optional).

CREAM STYLE CHICKEN ENCHILADAS

6 large flour tortillas
1 c. sour cream
1 10-¾ oz. can cream of chicken soup
1 7 oz. can diced green chiles
¾ lb Jack cheese
¾ lb. Cheddar cheese
1-½ c. cooked chicken cut into ½ inch cubes
½ tsp. salt

- Mix undiluted soup, sour cream, chicken, salt and green chiles together.
- Spread about 3 tbs. chicken mixture on a tortilla.
- Roll and lay seam side down in a 9 x 12 x 2 inch baking pan.
- Repeat with all tortillas, laying them close together.
- Grate cheeses to make 1 cup of each.
- Spread rest of chicken mixture over top of enchiladas in pan and sprinkle with mixed cheeses.
- Bake about 45 minutes in a 350 degree oven until hot and bubbly and cheese is melted.
- Serves 6, (or only 3, if you really like them!).

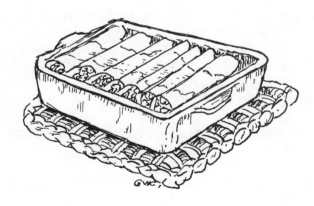

FIESTA CHICKEN

¾ c. milk
5 large chicken breasts
½ c. chicken broth
12 corn tortillas
1 lb. sharp Cheddar cheese
1 10-¾ oz. can cream of mushroom soup
1 10-¾ oz. can cream of chicken soup
1 15 oz. can chili without beans or 1-½ c. California Campfire Chili (see index)
1 7 oz. can diced green chiles

- Wrap chicken breasts securely in a large piece of aluminum foil folding in a seam across top and tucking in ends.
- Place in a large shallow pan and bake in a 350 degree oven for 1 hour, or until tender. Test by opening foil and piercing chicken with a fork.
- Save broth that has accumulated from chicken.
- Cool, bone, remove skins from chicken breasts. Cut into ½ inch cubes.
- Pour broth (there should be about ½ cup) in a deep 9 x 12 inch baking pan.
- Cut tortillas with a scissors into 1 inch squares.
- Grate cheese to make about 2 cups.
- Mix together the undiluted soups, chili without beans, green chiles and the milk. Stir well.
- Layer half the tortilla pieces in the chicken broth in the baking pan, then a layer of half the cheese and a layer of half the sauce.
- Repeat all layers, ending with cheese on top.
- Cover and refrigerate overnight. (This may also be frozen at this point.)
- When ready to bake, let stand in room temperature 1 hour before baking, if refrigerated.
- If frozen, thaw well before baking.
- Bake uncovered at 300 degrees for 1 hour until cheese is well melted and casserole is bubbly.
- Serves 6 to 8.

FRESH SALSA

2 large tomatoes
1 large red onion
1 4 oz. can diced green chiles
1 tbs. wine vinegar
1 tbs. olive oil
½ tsp. salt
½ tsp. sugar

- Peel and coarsely chop tomatoes.
- Peel and finely chop onion.
- Mix tomatoes and onion.
- Add chiles, wine vinegar, olive oil, sugar and salt.
- Mix well and refrigerate, covered.
- This fresh sauce will keep up to a week stored, covered, in the refrigerator.

Serve as an accompaniment in a Mexican meal, or as a first course or appetizer with tortilla chips. If one prefers a more zesty flavor, one may add a few drops hot liquid sauce, to taste.

GUACAMOLE SPEARS

1 lb. fresh asparagus
2 large tomatoes
6 green onions
½ tsp. salt
1 small lemon
2 medium avocados
1 tbs. mayonnaise
1 tbs. olive oil
4 drops liquid hot pepper sauce
Lettuce

- Peel and cook asparagus in ½ c. boiling water until firm tender, about 5 minutes. Drain and chill.
- Peel and dice tomatoes.
- Peel and chop 3 inches of onions, including part of the green tops.
- Squeeze lemon to make 1 tbs. juice.
- Mix tomatoes, onions, salt, lemon juice, mayonnaise, oil and hot pepper sauce to taste. Mix Guacamole and chill.
- Peel, discard seed and dice avocados just before serving. Add to Guacamole sauce and toss gently.
- Serve over cold cooked asparagus spears on a bed of shredded lettuce.
- Serves 4.

Hint: When cleaning fresh asparagus, cut off the top 5 inches to cook and serve as a vegetable or in the above recipe. Slice the remainder of the asparagus spears in ¾ inch slices until too tough to be palatable. Cook these asparagus spears until just tender, to be used either as a separate vegetable, or as a basis for creamed asparagus soup.

INDISPENSABLE GUACAMOLE

There are many variations of guacamole. In Mexican cooking, it is very adaptable, as an hors d'oeuvre, or in combination with other dishes. It can be spread, dipped into and poured over. It is mild, colorful, and delicious.

2 large ripe avocados
1 medium yellow onion
1 4 oz. can chopped green chiles
3 medium tomatoes
1 tbs. red chile powder, or to taste
1 medium lemon
1-½ tsp. sugar
½ tsp. garlic powder

- Squeeze lemon to make 2 tbs.
- Peel and lightly mash avocados.
- Peel and finely chop onion to make ⅓ cup.
- Peel, seed and coarsely chop tomatoes to make ⅔ cup.
- Mix mashed avocados, onion, diced chile, tomatoes, chile powder, juice of lemon, sugar and garlic powder.
- Chill before serving.
- Makes about 1-½ cup.

LIVER AND ONION OLE

4 tbs. butter
¾ tsp. salt
¼ tsp. pepper
1 large yellow onion
1 lb. sliced beef or calf liver
3 tbs. flour
⅓ c. Glad's Chili sauce (or any commercial cocktail chili sauce)
¼ oz. can diced green chiles
¾ lb. Jack cheese

- Peel and chop onion. Fry in butter until soft and golden, about 6 minutes. Remove from pan. Keep warm over low heat.
- Shred cheese to make about 1 cup.
- Cut membrane from liver and cut into serving size pieces.
- Sprinkle both sides of meat with flour, salt and pepper.
- Fry in the same skillet, adding a litle more butter if necessary.
- Fry about 3 minutes each side. Do not overcook.
- Remove to a heat proof plate, to keep warm.
- When ready to serve, place liver pieces on a broiler pan.
- Spread each serving piece with chili sauce, cooked onion and green chiles.
- Sprinkle cheese on top.
- Broil 4 inches from flame until bubbly and cheese is melted, about 4 minutes.
- Serve at once with rice or hominy sauteed in melted butter.
- Serves 4.

MEXICAN POT ROAST

3 lb. beef pot roast
2 tbs. oil
1 8 oz. can tomatoes
1 4 oz. can diced chiles
½ envelope taco seasoning mix
2 tsp. beef bouillon granules
1 tsp. sugar
¼ c. water

- Brown beef in a large pot roast pot or a dutch oven. Brown all sides.
- Cut up tomatoes. Combine tomatoes and their liquid with green chiles, water, dry taco mix, bouillon granules and sugar. Mix well.
- Pour over browned meat in pot and simmer, covered, for at least 2 hours.
- Turn once or twice, adding a bit more water if needed.
- Serve sliced, with corn fritters (see index) and juices from roast.
- Serves 6.

Records show that in nineteen hundred and ten California began chile pepper production.

NOGALES SALAD

1 12 oz. can whole kernel corn
1 small yellow or red onion
1 tsp. chile powder
½ tsp. salt
2 large ripe avocados
1 small lemon
4 tbs. mayonnaise
4 tbs. sour cream
1 medium green pepper
1 2 oz. jar pimento pieces
Lettuce

- Drain corn.
- Peel and chop onion.
- Wash, remove seeds and membrane from green pepper and chop.
- Mix corn, green pepper, chile powder and salt.
- Halve, peel and seed avocados.
- Squeeze lemon juice over avocado meat sparingly.
- Fill each avocado half with corn mixture.
- Shred lettuce.
- Mix mayonnaise and sour cream
- Place corn filled avocado halves on a bed of shredded lettuce.
- Top with 2 tbs. of the mayonnaise and sour cream dressing.
- Serves 4.

OVEN CHILE RELLENOS

½ lb. ground beef
½ lb. ground pork
1 tsp. bacon grease
1 large red onion
1 clove garlic
1 7 oz. can whole green chiles
1 lb. Cheddar cheese
1 tsp. salt
¼ tsp. hot pepper seasoning
4 eggs
¼ c. flour
1-½ c. milk

- Grate cheese to make 2 cups.
- Wash and remove seeds from chiles. Open up book fashion.
- Peel and chop onion.
- Peel and mince garlic.
- Brown meat in a large skillet in bacon grease. Add onion and garlic and cook mixture until onion is limp, about 5 minutes.
- Line an 8 x 8 x 2-½ inch baking pan with half the whole chiles.
- Top with 1-½ cups cheese.
- Spread brown crumbled meat over the cheese and then the rest of the chiles over the meat.
- Beat eggs. Mix flour, milk, salt and hot pepper seasoning.
- Add eggs and beat well.
- Pour egg mixture over contents of pan.
- Sprinkle with rest of cheese.
- Bake 350 degrees for 45 minutes, uncovered.
- Let stand 5 minutes in the baking pan before cutting to serve.
- Chile Relleno, served with a green vegetable, like broccoli, and sliced tomatoes with a small amount of salsa over them, makes a quick and tasty meal.

QUESO CALIENTE DIP

1 small yellow onion
1 tbs. cooking oil
1 12 oz. can stewed tomatoes
1 4 oz. can diced green chiles
3 drops hot pepper sauce
½ lb. sharp Cheddar cheese

- Peel and finely chop onion.
- Cook in oil in a skillet about 5 minutes until golden and soft.
- Add 1 cup tomatoes and diced chiles. Cook 3 minutes.
- Coarsely grate cheese and add to hot tomato mixture, along with a few drops of hot pepper sauce, to taste.
- Stir and cook until cheese is melted and sauce is hot.
- Serve hot, preferably in a small chafing dish. Use tortilla chips or small pieces of peeled jicama, a Mexican vegetable somewhat like a large turnip, for dipping.

REFRIED BEANS

2 c. Basic Beans (see index)
2 tbs. bacon drippings
¼ c. water or bean juice
¼ c. salsa (see index)
¼ lb. sharp Cheddar cheese

- Mash cooked beans with a potato masher.
- Fry beans in bacon grease over very low heat in a large skillet, stirring constantly. Add more liquid, water or bean juice, if beans stick to pan.
- Grate cheese to make about ½ cup.
- Add salsa and cheese to refried beans.
- Stir until cheese is melted and beans are bubbling hot.
- Refried beans are used as a constant accompaniment to most Southwestern dinners, or rolled in a warm flour tortilla to make a quick "Burrito."

SOUTHWESTERN CHEESE ENCHILADAS

8 corn tortillas
3 tbs. vegetable oil
2 10 oz. cans enchilada sauce
1 lb. sharp Cheddar cheese
24 green onions

- Grate cheese to make about 2-½ cups.
- Peel green onions and slice thin crosswise, using 2 to 3 inches of the stem section as well as the onion.
- Pour 1 can enchilada sauce in a pie plate.
- Heat oil in a large skillet. Dip tortillas one at a time in the hot oil for 5 seconds until limp, using kitchen tongs. Drip off oil and dip softened enchilada in enchilada sauce to cover. Stack on an oven proof plate. Keep warm in a low oven until all are covered with sauce.
- Taking one tortilla at a time, place ¼ c. grated cheese on each tortilla, along with a generous tbs. of sliced green onions.
- Roll each tortilla and lay seam side down in a 9 x 12 x 2 inch baking pan placing them close together.
- Spoon rest of enchilada sauce over the rolled tortillas and sprinkle with rest of cheese.
- Bake about 10 minutes in a 375 degree oven until cheese is melted and enchiladas are hot.
- Serves 4.

TOSTADA DE POLLO
(CHICKEN TOSTADAS)

4 corn tortillas
1 lb. sharp Cheddar cheese
4 medium tomatoes
2 medium yellow onions
2 c. cooked chopped chicken
1 10 oz. can enchilada sauce, or 1 c. Carmelita Huevos
   Rancheros sauce (see index)
Salsa

- Peel and chop tomatoes.
- Peel and chop onions.
- Grate cheese to make 1-½ to 2 cups.
- Place 4 tortillas flat in a large shallow baking pan.
- Spread each tortilla with 1 tbs. enchilada sauce, then sprinkle each with cheese, tomatoes, onion and chicken, adding another tbs. sauce over chicken. Sprinkle last of the cheese on top of each.
- Bake uncovered in a 350 degree oven until cheese melts, about 10 to 12 minutes. Edges of tortillas will begin to curl upward.
- Serve hot.
- Serves 2, or 4, if served along with a chili covered tamale.
- Pass more Rancheros sauce, heated, for an accompaniment, along with a dish of salsa.

SALADS

AVOCADO IN JELLIED BROTH
APPLESAUCE RASPBERRY SALAD
BABY SEA SHELL SALAD
CALIFORNIA COLE SLAW
GERMAN POTATO SALAD
GLAD'S SPECIAL CHICKEN SALAD
JICAMA SALAD
PEARL ONION SALAD
SAUERKRAUT SALAD
SEVEN-UP APPLESAUCE SALAD
SHRIMP CURRY SALAD
SOUR CREAM CUCUMBERS
SO EASY PARSLEY SALAD
SPINACH SALAD

SALAD DRESSINGS

MOM'S SALAD DRESSING
SPINACH SALAD DRESSING
TANGY ROQUEFORT CHEESE DRESSING

AVOCADO IN JELLIED BROTH

1 envelope unflavored gelatin
2 c. V-8 juice
1 c. beef broth, undiluted
1 tbs. Worcestershire sauce
3 drops hot sauce
1 large avocado
¾ c. sour cream

- Mix V-8 juice, broth and Worcestershire in a shallow bowl.
- Sprinkle gelatin evenly over the mixture. Let stand 5 minutes until it is softened. Mix and pour into a pan. Heat, stirring.
- Add hot sauce to taste.
- Pour into a bowl and chill until syrupy, about ½ hour.
- Peel and dice avocado and add to mixture. Mix gently.
- Chill until firm, 3 hours or more.
- Serve topped with sour cream, either alone or on shredded lettuce.
- Serves 4.

APPLESAUCE RASPBERRY SALAD

1 3 oz. pkg. raspberry jello
1 c. boiling water
1 10 oz. pkg. frozen raspberries
1 c. applesauce
5 oz. cream cheese
3 tbs. fruit juice

- Dissolve jello in boiling water.
- Add frozen raspberries, with their juice.
- Stir until berries are thawed.
- Stir in applesauce. Chill until firm, 3 hours or more.
- Wash and shred lettuce, if desired.
- Mash cream cheese at room temperature. Thin with fruit juice to desired dressing consistency. Serve over salad. Nice as an accompaniment to the main course, or on a bed of lettuce, for a salad.

BABY SEA SHELL SALAD

½ lb. baby sea shell pasta
3 c. boiling water
1 tsp. salt
¼ c. mayonnaise
2 tbs. chopped sweet pickle relish
1 2 oz. jar pimento pieces, or 1 small red bell pepper
2 green onions
2 tsp. horseradish
1 2-½ oz. can chopped black olives
3 celery stalks
¼ tsp. pepper

- Cook pasta in salted boiling water 7 to 10 minutes until firm tender, but not soft.
- Drain and wash with cold water. Place in a bowl.
- If using bell pepper, remove membranes and seeds and chop to make about 2 tbs.
- If using pimento, drain to make about 2 tbs.
- Chop celery to make about ½ cup. Peel and chop green onions to make 2 tbs. using 2 inches of bottom stems.
- Add mayonnaise, sweet pickle, pimento or red pepper, onion, horseradish, 2 tbs. chopped olives, pepper and celery to pasta. Mix well and chill.
- Serves 4 to 6.
- Shrimp, tuna or crab, may be added for a gourmet touch. Serves 8 to 10.

CALIFORNIA COLE SLAW

5 tbs. mayonnaise
2 tbs. prepared mustard
2 tbs. sugar
2 tbs. honey
2 tbs. vinegar
4 tbs. sour cream
1 tsp. caraway seed
1 tsp. horseradish
1 medium head cabbage

- To make the dressing, blend mustard, sugar, honey, vinegar and caraway seed.
- Add horseradish to mayonnaise. Mix well.
- Mix mayonnaise with honey and vinegar mixture.
- Store in refrigerator in a covered jar. Makes about ¾ pint of dressing.
- Finely shred cabbage.
- Just before serving, add dressing to cabbage to taste, and toss well.
- Not necessary, but for a gourmet touch, add ½ lb. cooked medium shrimp to slaw. Surprise!

GERMAN POTATO SALAD

3 lbs. White Rose or red potatoes
6 slices bacon
1 large yellow or red onion
1 tsp. salt
1-½ tbs. sugar
¼ tsp. pepper
½ c. vinegar
¼ c. water
½ tsp. celery seed
4 parsley sprigs

- Peel and chop onion.
- Wash parsley. Discard stems and chop flowerets to make about 3 tbs.
- Dice bacon and fry in a medium skillet until golden over medium heat, about 8 minutes.
- Remove all but 3 tbs. bacon grease from pan, saving rest of drippings for other uses.
- Add onion, cook 10 minutes, until it is golden.
- Add vinegar, water, salt and pepper. Stir. Set sauce aside.
- If using white potatoes, peel, cutting in half if too large, and boil until firm tender, about 15 minutes. Drain. Cool to room temperature.
- Slice thin into a large bowl.
- If using red potatoes, boil in their jackets until firm tender, about 20 to 25 minutes, depending upon their size.
- Drain and cool to room temperature. Peel. Slice thin into a large bowl.
- Pour warmed bacon mixture over still warm sliced potatoes. Add parsley and celery seed, tossing gently to mix. Serve warm, or at room temperature.
- For gourmet touch, peel and slice thin 1 cucumber, soaked in 1 tsp. salt dissolved in water to cover the cucumber slices, for about half an hour. Rinse in cold water. Drain and add to potato salad just before serving.
- This may be made a day ahead and kept refrigerated, covered.
- Warm slightly before serving.
- Serves 6.

So good with hot dogs or big German sausages. Great for a picnic because it does not have to be kept cold to be tasty.

GLAD'S SPECIAL CHICKEN SALAD

3 chicken breasts
½ c. mayonnaise
1 celery stalk and center and tender leaves of bunch
1 tsp. horseradish
1 c. seedless white grapes
1 11 oz. can mandarin oranges
½ tsp. salt
¼ tsp. pepper
½ c. dry currants

- Fold chicken breasts securely in aluminum foil, leaving a little air space for steam to gather under top folding seam.
- Bake about one hour in a 350 degree oven or until fork tender. Open foil to test. Be careful of steam. Save clear broth for other uses.
- Cool. Remove meat from bones. Discard bones and skin.
- Cut white meat of chicken into ½ inch chunks, placing in a large bowl.
- Chop celery stalk and tender heart and leaf tops to make about ¾ cup.
- Wash and remove stems from grapes.
- Add celery, horseradish, mayonnaise, salt and pepper to taste, to chicken.
- Mix to coat well. Add grapes and oranges last. Toss gently.
- Serve on shredded lettuce. Sprinkle currants over mounds of chicken for color and taste.
- A teaspoon of Glad's Orange Cranberry sauce (see index) on top of each serving really gives this salad a special tang and color.
- Serves 4.

JICAMA SALAD

Jicama is defined as ''the large white fleshy root of a Mexican vine.'' It looks like a sugar beet or a giant turnip. It can now be found in almost any supermarket, when it is in season.

1 l-lb. jicama
¼ c. white vinegar
2 tbs. sugar
Fresh mint leaves, or dried mint leaves

- Peel jicama and coarsely shred or cut into thin strips or grate on the coarse section of a grater, to make about 4 cups.
- Stir sugar and vinegar together until sugar is dissolved.
- Place jicama in a large salad bowl and pour vinegar and sugar mixture over it. Mix well and chill.
- Cut up fresh mint leaves with a scissors in small pieces to make about ½ cup and add, about ½ hour before serving. Toss well and keep chilled until ready to serve.
- If fresh mint is not available, mix jicama with dried crushed mint leaves.
- Serves 6 to 8.

PEARL ONION SALAD

**24 small white boiling onions (about 1-½ c.), or 1 16 oz.
   can baby white onions
1 envelope unflavored gelatin
½ c. cold water
¾ c. pineapple juice
1 c. boiling water
1 small lemon
¾ c. sugar
1 15 oz. can chunk pineapple
1 c. sliced blanched almonds
2 oz. jar pimento pieces, or 1 small red bell pepper
2 tbs. capers (optional)
2 tbs. vinegar
¼ tsp. salt**

- If fresh onions are used: Peel and cook in boiling water until just firm tender.
- If canned onions are used: Drain and remove any outer skin pieces, if tough.
- Squeeze lemon to make 1 tbs. juice.
- If using bell pepper: Remove membranes and seeds from pepper and coarsely chop to make ½ cup.
- Drain pimento pieces, if using pimentos.
- Dissolve gelatin with 1 c. boiling water. Cool.
- Add ½ c. pineapple juice, lemon juice and sugar to gelatin.
- When gelatin is partly set, about 20 minutes, add onion, blanched almonds, pimento or red pepper and pineapple chunks. Add vinegar, to taste.
- Add capers, if desired.
- Chill until firm, 3 hours or longer.
- Serve with a dressing made with mayonnaise thinned with ¼ c. pineapple juice.
- Serves 4.

Hint: When peeling small white onions, hold them under a slow stream of water to avoid eye irritation.

SAUERKRAUT SALAD

1 1-lb.-13 oz. can sauerkraut
2 medium yellow onions
4 or 5 celery stalks
2 medium green peppers
1 c. cider vinegar
2 c. sugar
½ tsp. salt, or to taste
¼ tsp. pepper, or to taste
Radishes and whole black pitted olives for garnish

- Drain sauerkraut, squeezing out as much juice as possible.
- Wash, remove membranes and seed from green peppers. Chop to make 1 cup.
- Peel and wash onions. Chop to make 1 cup.
- Wash and chop celery to make 1 cup.
- Wash and slice radishes.
- Combine sauerkraut, onions, celery, green pepper, vinegar and sugar.
- Mix well. Refrigerate, covered, for at least 24 hours.
- When ready to serve, drain some of the juice that has collected in the bowl, if necessary.
- Add salt and pepper to taste.
- This keeps several weeks in the refrigerator. It may be served as a salad. Or as an appetizer, in small appetizer dishes, with a small fork.
- Decorate the salad or individual servings with slices of red radishes and black olives.
- Serves 8.

SEVEN UP APPLESAUCE SALAD

7 oz. Seven Up
1 pkg. raspberry jello
1 c. applesauce
1 orange

- Heat applesauce.
- Dissolve jello in hot applesauce. Stir well.
- Grate rind of orange to make 2 tbs.
- Squeeze orange to make 2 tbs. of juice.
- Add orange juice and grated rind to jello mixture. Add Seven Up.
- Stir well.
- Chill until firm, 3 hours or more.
- Serves 4.

This is delicious either served alone or as a basis for a fruit salad.

SHRIMP CURRY SALAD

1 lb. (2 cups) cooked shrimp
2 cups firm tender cooked peas
6 stalks celery
½ c. chutney
1-½ tsp. salt
1 tsp. curry powder
⅓ c. sugar
⅓ c. olive oil
2 tbs. vinegar
Lettuce

- Thinly slice celery stalks crosswise to make 2 cups.
- Mix sugar, oil and vinegar to make dressing.
- In a large bowl combine shrimp, rice, peas, celery and chutney, salt and curry powder. Mix well.
- Pour ¾ cup dressing over rice and shrimp mixture.
- Toss well. Chill. Serve on shredded lettuce.
- Serves 4.

Goes well with cold sliced ham, pork, or corned beef for a summer luncheon.

SOUR CREAM CUCUMBERS

4 medium cucumbers
1 tsp. salt
¾ c. vinegar
1 c. sour cream
¼ tsp. coarsely ground pepper
Paprika

- Peel cucumbers and slice thin, leaving green strips of skin on for color, if desired.
- Sprinkle with salt. Let stand in a bowl for about 2 hours.
- Wash salt off, pressing out juice from slices.
- Pour vinegar over slices and refrigerate, covered, until 1 hour before serving.
- Pour off vinegar and mix in the sour cream stirring slices gently to cover. Season with pepper to taste, and more salt if necessary.
- Sprinkle with paprika.
- Serves 6.

You may prepare onion rings this way. Red onions are best, peeled and sliced thin. So good.

SO EASY PARSLEY SALAD

1 bunch parsley
1 4-½ oz. can chopped black olives
¼ c. olive oil
½ c. Parmesan cheese, or to taste

- Wash parsley, cutting off stems and pat flowerets dry.
- Pile into a serving bowl. Cut flowerets with a scissors into bite size pieces.
- Add chopped olives. Sprinkle with Parmesan cheese and olive oil.
- Toss well.
- Serve cold.
- Serves 4.

A perfect accompaniment to Italian pasta.

Hint: Keep parsley fresh and crisp by storing in a wide mouth jar with a tight lid, in the refrigerator. Parsley may also be frozen.

SPINACH SALAD

1 bunch fresh spinach
6 to 8 fresh white mushrooms
4 slices bacon
1 hard boiled egg
¼ c. walnut meats
Special Spinach Salad dressing (see index)

- Wash spinach thoroughly, removing stems and tearing leaves into bite size pieces.
- Drain in a large colander.
- Dry with paper towels, squeezing as much water from leaves as possible.
- Refrigerate in a salad bowl until ready to serve.
- Peel and coarsely chop egg, to make about 2 tbs.
- Finely chop walnuts to make 2 tbs.
- Wash mushrooms. Pat dry. Slice in thin slices.
- Cut bacon in ¼ inch pieces crosswise and fry until crisp. Remove and drain on a paper towel. Save bacon drippings for other uses.
- Just before serving, add bacon pieces, mushrooms, walnuts and egg to spinach.
- Pour about ¼ c. Special Spinach Dressing over all and toss lightly and thoroughly.
- Serves 4.

MOM'S SALAD DRESSING

1 10-½ oz. can tomato soup
¾ c. olive oil
¼ c. vinegar
2 tbs. sugar
1 tsp. dry mustard
1 tsp. paprika
1 tsp. Worcestershire sauce
1-½ tsp. salt
½ tsp. pepper
2 cloves
1/8 tsp. garlic powder
1 small white onion

- Peel and finely chop enough onion to make about 2 tbs.
- Put onions, tomato soup undiluted, olive oil, vinegar, sugar, mustard, paprika, Worcestershire sauce, salt, pepper, cloves and garlic powder in a quart jar.
- Cover, shake well to mix and let stand covered in the refrigerator a day or two. Shake well before serving.
- Good on sliced tomatoes, or sliced cucumbers. This dressing is an all purpose dressing, nice to have on hand.

SPINACH SALAD DRESSING

2 tbs. olive oil
1 tsp. vinegar
½ tsp. Dijon mustard
4 tbs. pineapple juice
2 tsp. brown sugar
¼ tsp. salt
Dash of coarse pepper

- Mix olive oil, vinegar, mustard, pineapple juice, brown sugar, salt and pepper in a covered bottle or jar.
- Shake thoroughly.
- Store in refrigerator. Shake again before using.
- Makes about ¼ cup.

Best on Spinach Salad (see index).

TANGY ROQUEFORT CHEESE DRESSING

¼ **lb. Roquefort or Blue cheese (4 oz.)**
½ **c. mayonnaise**
½ **c. sour cream**
¼ **tsp. pepper**
¼ **tsp. dry mustard**
1 **tsp. horseradish**
1 **small lemon**
½ **tsp. sugar**

- Mash cheese.
- Squeeze lemon to make 1 tbs. juice.
- Mix mayonnaise, sour cream, pepper, mustard, horseradish and lemon juice in a mixing bowl.
- Fold in cheese last. Mix well.
- Keeps well in a covered jar in the refrigerator.
- Makes about ¾ pint.

SOUPS

SACRAMENTO CLAM CHOWDER
LIMA BEAN SOUP
VICHYSSOISE

SACRAMENTO CLAM CHOWDER

3 bacon slices
1 large white onion
3 medium White Rose potatoes
1 tsp. salt
¼ tsp. pepper
1-½ c. water
Dash of liquid hot sauce
2 c. milk
1 tbs. butter
3 6-½ oz. cans chopped clams
3 tbs. water
3 tbs. flour

- Dice bacon.
- Peel and chop onion.
- Peel and cube potatoes in ½ inch cubes.
- Saute bacon pieces in a large deep skillet until nearly crisp.
- Add onion and cook until golden and tender, about 8 minutes.
- Add salt, pepper, potatoes and water.
- Cook 10 minutes or until potatoes are tender but not mushy.
- Add chopped clams with their liquid, milk, butter and a dash of hot sauce.
- Cook 3 minutes.
- Thicken to consistency of your choice with water and flour mixed together.
- Serves 6.

This is a wonderful soup to serve steaming hot in Crust Bowls (see index). It becomes a conversational lunch. Break the edges of the bowl to dip into the soup. Serve with Sour Cream cucumbers (see index) or Jicama Salad (see index) as an accompaniment.

If you have a crock pot, keeping the soup hot in the pot is an easy way to serve it, using a long handled soup ladle to ladle it into warm bowls right at the table.

LIMA BEAN SOUP

6 slices bacon
2 medium yellow onions
6 stalks celery
2 medium carrots
1 lb. large white dried lima beans
3 qts. water
1 tsp. salt
1 tsp. liquid hot pepper sauce, or to taste
½ tsp. thyme
2 bay leaves
3 ham hocks

- Dice bacon and saute in a large skillet until soft, about 5 minutes. Remove bacon pieces.
- Coarsely chop celery to make 1 cup.
- Peel and slice onions to make 1 cup.
- Peel and dice carrots to make ½ cup.
- Wash beans.
- Saute onions and carrots in bacon grease until lightly browned. Place bacon, beans, water, celery, carrots, salt, pepper, thyme, bay leaves and ham hocks in a large kettle. Bring to a gentle boil, covered, then simmer 2-½ to 3 hours until beans are soft and very tender. Add more water if needed.
- Discard bay leaves. Remove ham hocks and cut off meat into small pieces.
- Discard bones.
- Return meat to soup and add hot sauce to taste, a dash will do.
- Serve hot, with One-Two-Three bread (see index).

VICHYSSOISE

There are many different recipes for this cold soup, served as an appetizer or first course — beautiful and tantilizing. It is an elegant addition to any meal. This recipe is simple, and well worth the effort.

To me, Vichyssoise conjures up images of soft candlelight and intimate dinners. The dictionary defines it as simply ''a thick creamy soup made of delectably cooked potatoes, onions and spices.'' It may also be enjoyed on a warm summer day, poured from a thermos into a mug on a picnic. It is best made with leeks, but firm white onions may be used.

3 leeks or medium white onions
4 tbs. water
4 or 5 medium White Rose potatoes
2 pints Half and Half cream
1 tsp. salt
½ tsp. white pepper
3 green onions for garnish

- Cut leeks into very thin slices to make 3 cups.
- Cook in water until soft, about 5 minutes.
- Finely slice green onions, using 2 inches of their tops, to make about 3 or 4 tsps.
- Peel and coarsely grate potatoes to make 4 cups.
- Add to onions and any remaining liquid. Add a little more water if necessary.
- Simmer 20 minutes until potatoes are soft. Stir occasionally to prevent burning.
- Puree potatoes and onions through a food mill into a bowl.
- Add 2 cups of Half and Half cream. Salt and pepper to taste.
- Chill, covered, 4 hours or overnight.
- Best served in a chilled plate or cup, sprinkled with sliced green onions for garnish. Serve with Flaky Stix (see index).
- Serves 4.

CAKES

APPLESAUCE CAKE
MOCHA FROSTING
HOT MILK CAKE WITH COCONUT TOPPING
INVERTED CRANBERRY CAKE
SPANISH BUN CAKE
WHITE FRUIT CAKE

APPLESAUCE CAKE

½ c. shortening
1·⅓ c. sugar
2 eggs
1·½ c. thick applesauce
1 c. raisins
½ c. chopped walnuts
4 tbs. hot water
2 c. flour
½ tsp. salt
1 tsp. cinnamon
2 tsp. baking soda
1/8 tsp. cloves
½ tsp. nutmeg

- Cream sugar and shortening. Beat eggs. Add to creamed mixture.
- Add applesauce, nuts and raisins. Mix well.
- Add water. Beat.
- Mix flour, cinnamon, baking soda, cloves and nutmeg. Add to batter.
- Beat well.
- Spoon into a greased 10 inch tube pan, a loaf pan, or two 9 inch layer pans.
- Bake in a 350 degree oven 1 hour and 10 minutes if using a tube pan; about 1 hour if using a loaf pan; or 45 minutes if making layers; until a cake tester thrust in center comes out clean.
- Cool in the pan 5 minutes and then invert on a rack to cool further.
- When cool, remove to a serving plate to frost.
- Mocha frosting (see index) is perfect for this cake.
- Or — serve cake warm — with warm Soft Sauce (see index) poured over each individual serving.

MOCHA FROSTING

2 c. powdered sugar
1 cube butter
1 tbs. instant coffee, or to taste
2 tbs. hot water

- Cream sugar and butter together until smooth.
- Dissolve coffee in hot water to make strong syrup.
- Add syrup to sugar mixture, 1 tsp. at a time, mixing until frosting becomes spreadable.
- This frosting is wonderful on any dark cake, especially Applesauce cake (see index). If a tube cake, cover completely with frosting. If layer cake, spread the frosting between the layers and over the top and sides.

Beautiful to eat and look at!

HOT MILK CAKE WITH COCONUT TOPPING

BATTER

2 eggs
¼ tsp. salt
1 c. sugar
1 c. flour
½ c. milk
1-½ tsp. baking powder
1 tbs. butter
½ tsp. lemon flavoring
½ tsp. vanilla flavoring

TOPPING

½ c. butter
3 tbs. evaporated milk
1 c. brown sugar
1 c. shredded coconut

- Beat eggs. Add sugar, salt and flavorings. Beat.
- Heat milk and butter together until butter is melted. Do not boil.
- Add to egg and sugar mix. Mix well.
- Add flour and baking powder. Beat.
- Pour quickly into a greased 9 x 10 x 2-½ inch baking pan.
- Bake at 350 degrees for 25 minutes. Mix butter, evaporated milk, brown sugar and coconut to make topping.
- Spread on hot baked cake, after the cake has cooled on a wire rack 5 minutes.
- Place under broiler, about 3 inches from heat, until topping is golden and bubbly, about 5 minutes, or only until brown. Watch carefully so topping does not burn.
- Serve warm.

INVERTED CRANBERRY CAKE

½ c. sugar
1 lb. fresh cranberries, about 2 cups
¾ cube butter
½ c. sugar
1 egg
1 tsp. vanilla
1 small orange
1-¼ c. flour
1-½ tsp. baking powder
¼ tsp. salt
½ c. milk
2 tbs. sugar

- Grate rind of orange to make a full tsp.
- Cream butter and sugar.
- Beat egg. Add egg, vanilla and grated orange rind to creamed mixture.
- Mix flour, baking powder and salt.
- Add to creamed mixture alternately with milk. Beat well.
- Butter a 9 x 9 x 1-½ inch cake pan.
- Sprinkle sugar over bottom of pan.
- Wash, rinse and dry cranberries and spread over sugar in pan.
- Pour batter over cranberries.
- Bake on a baking sheet in a 350 degree oven for one hour or until well browned.
- Remove from oven and cool on a wire rack for ½ hour.
- Invert onto a serving plate.
- Serve with ice cream or whipped cream.

SPANISH BUN CAKE

½ c. butter
1 c. brown sugar
2 eggs
¼ tsp. baking powder
½ c. sour milk or buttermilk
½ tsp. baking soda
1 c. and 2 tbs. flour
½ tsp. each vanilla, cinnamon, cloves and allspice
1 c. chopped walnuts
1 c. brown sugar

- Cream butter and sugar.
- Separate eggs. Beat yolks.
- Add yolks to creamed mixture. Beat. Add vanilla. Beat.
- Mix baking powder, baking soda, flour ,cinnamon, cloves and allspice together.
- Add alternately with sour milk to creamed mixture. Beat well. Pour into 2 greased cake layer pans.
- Beat egg whites until stiff.
- Add the beaten whites to sugar gradually, folding in well. Add half the nuts.
- Stir gently to mix.
- Spread on top of the batter in the 2 cake layer pans.
- Sprinkle rest of nuts on top of each.
- Bake at 350 degrees for 30 minutes. Be sure oven is not too hot.
- Remove from oven and let cool in the pans on a wire rack.
- Cut in squares, if using single layers. Or layer the squares and put ice cream between them for a very special dessert.

WHITE FRUIT CAKE

1 c. sugar
1 c. flour
1 tsp. baking powder
½ tsp. salt
¾ tsp. brandy
4 eggs
15 candied cherries
8 oz. jar candied pineapple slices
1 lb. whole dates
½ lb. whole walnut meats
½ lb. whole Brazil nuts

- Separate eggs. Beat yolks and whites separately.
- Mix together flour, sugar, baking powder and salt.
- Mix together beaten egg yolks, vanilla and brandy.
- Add egg yolk mixture to flour mixture. Fold in beaten whites last, to complete the batter.
- Cut pineapple slices into large pieces.
- Mix pineapple, whole pitted dates, whole cherries and whole nuts together.
- Douse fruit and nuts thoroughly with flour.
- Add floured fruit and nuts to cake batter.
- Pour into a well greased loaf pan.
- Bake at 350 degrees about 1 hour until a cake tester thrust in center comes out clean.
- Invert on a wire rack to cool. Wrap in wax paper for storing.
- Be sure and slice with a sharp knife to serve, so that you cut through the whole nuts and fruit. This makes a beautiful pattern in the slice, with just a little cake edging to hold the colorful contents together. Especially appropriate served with wine or Tom and Jerrys during the holidays.

SAUCES

BUTTERSCOTCH SAUCE
CURRY SAUCE
DI BELLA SPAGHETTI SAUCE
GLAD'S CHILI SAUCE
HOT CINNAMON SAUCE
MUSTARD SAUCE FOR HAM
LEMON SAUCE
SARA'S MOCK HOLLANDAISE SAUCE
SPECIAL STEAK MARINADE
SPRIGHTLY SAUCE
THICK AND TANGY TOMATO SAUCE

BUTTERSCOTCH SAUCE

4 c. (l lb.) brown sugar
1 12 oz. can evaporatd milk
¼ c. butter

- Melt butter in the top of a double boiler.
- Add brown sugar. Mix well.
- Stir in 1 c. evaporated milk slowly.
- Cook, covered, about ½ hour, stirring frequently to prevent sticking.
- Yummy over vanilla ice cream, apple pie, or custard pudding.
- Serve warm.
- Makes about 1-½ cups.

CURRY SAUCE

4 tbs. butter
4 tbs. flour
2·½ c. Half and Half cream
½ tsp. onion salt
¼ tsp. pepper
2 tsp. curry powder, or more to taste

- Melt butter in a large skillet. Stir in flour and cook, stirring, one minute until thoroughly mixed.
- Add Half and Half all at once, stirring constantly.
- Simmer, stirring, for 10 minutes until well thickened and smooth.
- Season with salt and pepper. Add curry last, stirring to mix thoroughly.
- Especially good on So Long Turkey patties (see index), as well as pasta, or baked white meat fish.
- Makes about 2 cups of sauce.

Hint: For a simple cream sauce, add ½ tsp. Worcestershire sauce to taste, instead of curry powder, for that little zest. Good on chipped beef or on leftover vegetables.

DI BELLA SPAGHETTI SAUCE

1 clove garlic
1 medium yellow onion
½ lb. fresh mushrooms
4 tbs. olive oil
2 16 oz. cans whole peeled tomatoes
1 15 oz. can tomato sauce
2 6 oz. cans tomato paste
2 tsp. sweet basil
½ tsp. oregano
1 tsp. Worcestershire sauce
2 tsp. salt
1 tsp. pepper
3 drops hot sauce
3 tbs. grated Parmesan cheese
5 sprigs fresh parsley

- Peel and mince garlic.
- Peel and finely chop onions.
- Wash, pat dry and slice mushrooms.
- Wash parsley. Discard stems. Chop flowerets fine to make about 4 tbs.
- Saute garlic and onion in olive oil in a large skillet until soft and golden, about 5 minutes.
- Add mushrooms and fry 2 more minutes, stirring.
- Mix tomatoes and their juice, tomato paste, basil, parsley, oregano, Worcestershire sauce, salt, pepper, hot sauce and Parmesan cheese.
- Add tomato mixture to mushrooms in skillet. Simmer about 1 hour, or until thick. Stir occasionally to prevent sticking.
- Makes about 1 qt. sauce. Store in a covered jar in the refrigerator.

GLAD'S CHILI SAUCE

This recipe originated in my grandmother's kitchen. For her, the name Chili Sauce did not bring to mind the use of the Mexican chile flavor, but rather a zesty mixture of tomatoes and spices! Today I have added a touch of Mexican chile, which I believe enhances the deep zest of the sauce.

You may make the original recipe if you prefer. Either way, I use this sauce extensively, as you might notice as you read through the recipes in this book. Left over pot roast or meat loaf slices are given new life warmed in a few tablespoonsful of Chili Sauce. And shrimp or crab cocktails become outstanding perked with a dab of horseradish and Glad's Chile sauce. Experiment for yourself. You may want to change proportions of spices to suit your individual taste.

1 peck ripe tomatoes (8 qts.)
12 medium yellow or red onions
6 large green peppers
2 c. sugar
1 pint vinegar (2 c.)
2 tbs. salt
**1-½ tbs. whole allspice, (I have used powdered allspice in
     a pinch, but it isn't as good)**
6 inches stick cinnamon
1 tbs. whole cloves
1 tsp. paprika

- Peel and quarter tomatoes. Peel and chop onions. Remove membranes and seeds and chop green peppers.
- Mix onions, green pepper, sugar and salt in a large bowl. Pour mixture into one very large cooking pot, or 2 medium pots.
- Tie allspice, stick cinnamon broken into smaller pieces, cloves and paprika, loosely in a little 5 inch square of porous cloth, pulled up at the corners to form a bag. Tie at the top with a 12 inch length of cotton string. Attach other end of string to handle of the cooking pot. If using 2 pots, make 2 bags, dividing the spices.
- Mash the bag with a long handled spoon occasionally while cooking, to urge out the flavor of the spices. Cook rapidly until tender, stirring often.
- It is at this point that I add 2 or more tbs. red chile powder, to taste.
- Add the vinegar, and cook rapidly until quite thick, about 1-½ hours.
- Stir often to prevent sticking.
- Fill hot sterilized jars to ½ inch of the top. Seal at once.

HOT CINNAMON SAUCE

⅓ c. sugar
3 tbs. flour
1 c. water
1 large lemon
1 tbs. butter
½ tsp. cinnamon
¼ tsp. nutmeg

- Squeeze lemon to make 3 tbs. of juice.
- Mix sugar and flour in a small pan. Add water and lemon juice. Cook, stirring, until thickened.
- Add butter, cinnamon and nutmeg, mixing well.
- Serve warm over hot apple pie (see index).

MUSTARD SAUCE FOR HAM

½ c. melted butter
½ c. sugar
½ c. prepared mustard
1 10 oz. can tomato soup
½ c. vinegar
2 egg yolks

- Separate yolks and whites of eggs. (Save whites for other uses.)
- Slightly beat yolks.
- Melt butter in a cooking pot. Add sugar, mustard, undiluted soup, vinegar and egg yolks.
- Stir constantly while cooking over very low heat until slightly thickened.
- Serve warm or at room temperature with slices of cooked ham.
- Makes 1-½ cups. Store in refrigerator.

LEMON SAUCE

1 tbs. soy sauce
½ tsp. salt
½ tsp. pepper
¼ c. vegetable oil
3 large lemons
2 tbs. grated lemon peel
1 clove garlic

- Grate rind of lemons to make 2 tbs.
- Squeeze juice from lemons to make ½ cup.
- Peel and crush garlic clove.
- Mix soy sauce, salt, pepper, oil, garlic, lemon juice and grated lemon rind.
- Refrigerate at least 1 hour before using. Stir before applying as a marinade.
- A great marinade for oven baked chicken or fish.

SARA'S MOCK HOLLANDAISE SAUCE

There is a special story accompanying this recipe, about the cook at the St. George Hotel, in the old mining town of Volcano, California. She has held court there for many years, accentuating the unforgettable experience of enjoying dinner in ''her'' proud old dining room.

Sara hovers between the kitchen and the guests at the cloth covered tables, constantly darting in and out to keep a watchful eye on everyone. It is a never ceasing wonder how she manages being a wonderful cook and a very visual and gracious hostess, besides. She is eager to share her creations for the pure joy of it, with anyone who is interested. Hence — this recipe.

1 c., Miracle Whip, or mayonnaise
1 small lemon
¾ tsp. Dijon mustard
A "little" evaporated milk (1 to 2 tsp.)

- Squeeze lemon to make 1 tbs. juice. Add lemon juice slowly to mayonnaise, blending well.
- Add mustard and a "little" evaporated milk.
- Mix well.
- Plop 1 or 2 tbs. of this sauce on a cooked hot serving of fresh broccoli or asparagus, and watch your guests wonder!

SPECIAL STEAK MARINADE

¼ **c. soy sauce**
¼ **c. olive oil**
1 clove garlic
½ **tsp. ginger**
2 tbs. honey
2 tbs. vinegar
2 tbs. catsup

- Peel and mince garlic.
- Mix soy sauce, oil, garlic, ginger, honey, vinegar and catsup together.
- Pour into a bottle or jar with a top and shake well.
- Store in refrigerator until ready to use. Shake before pouring over steaks.
- Marinate steaks overnight, turning several times to coat meat thoroughly. (This sauce is also good on lamb, or chicken to barbecue or broil.)
- The steaks may be placed in a freezable container. Marinate for several hours before freezing.
- Great idea to take frozen meat in its frozen container on that "barbecue in the woods," or whatever, timing the thawing process to be ready to use when needed.
- Especially good on rolled "skirt steaks."

SPRIGHTLY SAUCE

3 tbs. butter
½ c. catsup
1 small lemon
1 tsp. Worcestershire sauce
1 tsp. prepared mustard
½ tsp. liquid hot pepper seasoning
2 tbs. Sherry wine

- Melt butter in small skillet.
- Squeeze lemon to make 1 tbs. juice.
- Stir in catsup, lemon juice, Worcestershire sauce, mustard and hot pepper seasoning.
- Bring just to a boiling point. Remove from heat and stir in Sherry wine slowly.
- This sauce is particularly good when used on Crab Fitters (see index).
- Use sparingly.

THICK AND TANGY TOMATO SAUCE

¼ c. vegetable oil
4 large yellow or red onions
1 16 oz. can whole tomatoes
2 8 oz. cans tomato paste
2 tsp. chile powder, or to taste
2 tbs. sugar
¾ tsp. garlic salt
½ tsp. black pepper

- Peel and chop onions to make 2 cups.
- Saute onions in a large heavy skillet about 5 minutes until softened.
- Stir in tomatoes with their juices, tomato paste, chile powder, sugar, vinegar, salt and pepper.
- Stir and bring to a boil, breaking up tomatoes.
- Cook slowly, uncovered, until sauce is of desired thickness and well blended, about 30 minutes. (The longer it simmers, the better it gets.)
- Remove from heat and taste for seasonings.
- This sauce keeps well, refrigerated, for several weeks.
- Serve hot over Corned Beef Roll Ups (see index).
- Makes about 1 pint of sauce.

BREADS

BANANA NUT BREAD
FLAKY STIX
POPPY SEED CRISPS

SANDWICHES

CRAB MELT
FORTY NINER CORNED BEEF SANDWICHES
HOME STYLE MONTE CRISTO
MUSHROOM AND SWISS CHEESE ON RYE
PIQUANT SHRIMP ROLLS

BANANA NUT BREAD

1-¾ c. flour
2 tsp. baking powder
¼ tsp. baking soda
½ tsp. salt
⅔ c. sugar
⅓ c. shortening
2 eggs
2 or 3 ripe bananas
½ c. chopped walnuts

- Mix flour, baking powder, baking soda and salt.
- Cream shortening. Add sugar gradually.
- Peel and mash bananas to make 1 cup.
- Beat eggs well. Add to creamed mixture.
- Add flour mixture alternately with mashed bananas to creamed mixture.
- Add nuts. Mix well.
- Turn into a well greased bread pan. Bake at 350 degrees about 1 hour, or until tester thrust in center comes out clean.
- Turn out on a wire rack to cool.
- This bread slices better when served the next day.
- Delicious toasted.

FLAKY STIX

Flaky Pie Crust dough (see index)
1 tsp. celery seeds
1 tsp. chile powder
4 tbs. butter

- Roll dough to about ¼ inch "thinness" on a floured board, using ½ the amount of the recipe and saving rest in refrigerator, well wrapped in plastic wrap. (It will keep 4 or 5 days.)
- Melt butter. Mix with celery seeds and chile powder.
- Brush on top of rolled sheet of dough with a pastry brush.
- Cut in 3 x 1 inch strips.
- Remove with a spatula to a cookie sheet and bake 10 minutes at 350 degrees until golden brown.
- Serve hot or cold with salads or soups. Also great as a quick appetizer.
- Store in a covered container.
- Makes about 20 strips.

POPPY SEED CRISPS

4 hot dog rolls
Soft butter
Grated Parmesan cheese
Poppy seeds

- Cut rolls lengthwise in halves and each half in half again, lengthwise.
- Butter each strip on exposed sides.
- Place strips on a cookie sheet and sprinkle buttered sides with Parmesan cheese and poppy seeds.
- Bake at 350 degrees about 10 minutes or until crisp and golden brown.
- These are a remarkable substitute when you don't have time to bake some "real" rolls for dinner.
- Serve warm.
- Makes 16 strips.

CRAB MELT

¼ c. mayonnaise
4 ¼ inch slices Swiss cheese
1 6 oz. can crab meat or ¼ lb. fresh crab meat
2 stalks celery
3 green onions
1 small green pepper
Salt and pepper to taste
Paprika
4 slices rye bread

- Finely chop celery to make 3 tbs.
- Peel and finely chop green onions, including 2 inches of stems to make 2 tbs.
- Remove membrane and seeds from green pepper and chop to make 2 tbs.
- Flake crab meat, removing any cartilage and bones.
- Mix crab meat, celery, onions and green pepper in a small bowl.
- Add mayonnaise. Salt and pepper to taste. Spread crab mixture on rye bread slices toasted on one side only.
- Place a slice of Swiss cheese on top of crab mixture. Sprinkle with paprika.
- Broil sandwiches 4 inches from heat until cheese is melted, salad is warm and rye bread toasted.
- Serve with potato or macaroni salad.

FORTY-NINER CORNED BEEF SANDWICHES

12 oz. can corned beef
¼ lb. sharp Cheddar cheese
1 5 oz. jar pimento stuffed green olives
⅓ c. tomato catsup
1 tsp. Worcestershire sauce
4 green onions
1 small green pepper
6 hot dog buns

- Shred corned beef.
- Shred cheese to make ¾ cup.
- Finely chop green onions to make 3 tbs.
- Remove membranes and seeds from green pepper and chop to make 2 tsp.
- Combine corned beef, cheese, green olives, onion and green pepper. Stir in catsup and Worcestershire sauce.
- Split rolls until almost separated. Scoop bread out of each half from inside bun.
- Fill with mixture and fold roll together again. Secure with toothpicks, if necessary.
- Wrap each stuffed roll in aluminum foil. Heat in a 325 degree oven for 20 minutes before serving.
- Roll should be hot and crispy and cheese melted.
- Serves 6.

HOME STYLE MONTE CRISTO

12 slices french bread
4 tbs. Dijon mustard
2 tbs. mayonnaise
6 slices cooked ham
6 slices Swiss cheese
2 eggs
½ tsp. salt
½ tsp. pepper
½ c. milk
4 tbs. butter
Bread and Butter pickles (see index)

- Mix mustard and mayonnaise.
- Spread each bread slice with mustard and mayonnaise.
- Place a slice of ham, a slice of cheese, on each piece of bread, topping with 2 or 3 pickle slices.
- Cover with another slice of bread.
- Beat eggs well. Mix in milk, salt and pepper.
- Dip each sandwich in egg mixture, coating both sides.
- Fry over low heat in melted butter, pressing down with a spatula to melt cheese. Turn to toast both sides. Add more butter if needed.
- This makes a hearty lunch combined with German potato salad (see index).

MUSHROOM AND SWISS CHEESE ON RYE

**1 large yellow onion
1 clove garlic
¾ lb. mushrooms
4 tbs. butter
6 slices rye bread
½ lb. Swiss cheese**

- Shred cheese to make about 1 cup.
- Peel and chop onion to make ½ cup.
- Peel and mince garlic.
- Wash, pat dry and slice mushrooms to make 1 cup to 1-½ cups.
- Slightly toast rye bread slices.
- Saute onion, garlic and mushrooms in butter until most of the liquid is evaporated.
- Place bread slices on a baking sheet.
- Pile sauteed mushrooms on each slice. Sprinkle with cheese.
- Broil about 4 inches from flame until cheese melts.
- Serves 3, (or 6, if combined with a salad on the same serving plate).

PIQUANT SHRIMP ROLLS

½ **lb. sharp Cheddar cheese**
1 **medium green pepper**
1 **c. pimento stuffed green olives**
4 **green onions**
½ **c. olive oil**
½ **c. tomato sauce**
¼ **lb. small cooked shrimp, or 2 4-½ oz. cans small shrimp**
8 **hot dog rolls**

- Grate cheese.
- Chop green pepper, after removing seeds and membrane.
- Peel and chop onions including 2 inches of the green stems.
- Mix cheese, green pepper, olives, onion, olive oil, tomato sauce and shrimp together.
- Cut rolls in half. Scoop out bread with a fork, leaving about ¼ inch shells.
- Butter inside of each shell, top and bottom. Fill with shrimp mixture.
- Put rolls back to fit. Secure with vertical toothpicks at each end.
- Wrap each roll in aluminum foil, folding over ends and securing foil.
- Bake on a cookie sheet in their foil jackets in a 350 degree oven for 20 minutes.
- Unwrap to serve. Place 2 rolls carefully on each individual serving plate.
- These may be prepared in advance and stored in the refrigerator until ½ hour before serving time. Heat oven in advance to 350 degrees.
- Bake rolls 20 minutes.
- Makes a delightful luncheon combined on the same plate with a small colorful fruit salad.
- Serves 4.

COOKIES

APRICOT COCONUT SQUARES
CHEWS
CHEWY NUT COOKIES
CHOCOLATE COCONUT KISSES
DANISH JAM COOKIES
MOLASSES KRINKLES
PEANUT BUTTER COOKIES
U.C. BROWNIES

DESSERTS

APPLE PIE
EVERYBODY KNOWS LEMON HEAVEN
FLAKY PIE CRUST
FLOATING ISLAND
GRAHAM CRACKER CRUMB SHELL
JAM TARTS
ROSEMARY APPLE PUDDING
WALNUT TORTE
SARA'S PEACHY DESSERT
SOUR CREAM CHEESE PIE

APRICOT COCONUT SQUARES

BATTER

¾ **cube butter**
1 **c. flour**
1 **tsp. baking powder**
1 **egg**
1 **tbs. milk**

TOPPING

8 **level tsp. apricot jam**
1 **egg**
1 **c. sugar**
4 **tbs. melted butter**
1 **tsp. vanilla**
2 **c. shredded coconut**

- Beat egg for batter.
- Mix egg, flour, baking powder and milk. Beat into a batter and pour in a greased 9 x 9 x 2 inch baking pan.
- Spread jam over batter.
- Beat egg and mix with sugar, melted butter, vanilla and coconut.
- Spread coconut mixture over batter and jam in pan.
- Bake at 350 degrees for 35 minutes or until nicely browned and a tester thrust in center comes out clean.
- Cut into squares in pan. Let cool 10 minutes before removing to a wire rack to cool completely.
- Delicious as a snack, or as a dessert.

CHEWS

1 c. brown sugar
1 c. coarsely chopped walnuts
1 egg
5 tbs. flour
¼ tsp. salt
1 scant tsp. baking soda

- Mix sugar and egg. Add walnuts.
- Mix flour, salt and soda. Add to blended sugar and egg.
- Place batter in a 9 x 9 x 2 inch greased baking pan. Batter will be very thick.
- Spread with a spoon to edges of pan.
- Bake 20 to 25 minutes at 325 degrees.
- Do not over bake. The Chews will be chewy on the inside and crisp on top. Cut while still hot in the pan, let stand 5 minutes and then remove squares with a spatula to a wire rack to cool.
- Store in a covered jar.
- This is a quick, easy and versatile recipe. Either cut into squares as snacks or in larger serving pieces topped with whipped cream or ice cream for dessert.
- Makes 16 squares.

WALNUT SNAPS

1 c. white sugar
1 c. brown sugar
½ c. shortening
2 eggs
1 tsp. vanilla flavoring
3 scant c. flour
1 tsp. baking powder
½ tsp. salt
1 c. finely chopped walnuts

- Cream shortening and sugar.
- Add eggs and vanilla. Mix well.
- Stir together flour, baking powder and salt. Add to creamed mixture.
- Mix, then add nuts and mix again.
- Take dough by heaping teaspoonful and shape into balls about the size of a large walnut. Put on a greased cookie sheet 1-½ inches apart.
- Flatten each ball with bottom of a butter greased glass dipped in sugar.
- Bake 10 to 12 minutes until edges are golden and crispy, in a 350 degree oven.
- Remove with a spatula to paper towels to cool.
- Makes about 3 dozen cookies.

CHOCOLATE COCONUT KISSES

3 eggs
1 c. sugar
3 heaping tsps. sweet chocolate powder
1 c. shredded coconut
1 tsp. vanilla

- Separate eggs. Beat whites until stiff. (Save yolks for other uses.)
- Add sugar and chocolate.
- Stir over heat thoroughly for 4 minutes, or until sugar is dissolved and thoroughly mixed with chocolate. Be careful not to burn.
- Stir in coconut and vanilla.
- Drop from a teaspoon onto a buttered cookie sheet.
- Bake in a 350 degree oven, 10 to 15 minutes.
- Remove with a spatula to a wire rack to cool.

DANISH JAM COOKIES

1 c. butter
½ c. sugar
2 eggs
2 c. flour
1 tsp. vanilla
Jam of your choice

- Separate eggs. (Save whites for other uses.)
- Beat egg yolks.
- Cream butter and sugar.
- Add egg yolks. Beat.
- Add flour. Mix well to form dough.
- Make balls by hand about the size of a large walnut. Flour hands if dough is too sticky.
- Place balls on a greased cookie sheet about 2 inches apart. Press an indention with finger in top of each. Fill the depression with jam, about ½ tsp. on each cookie.
- Bake at 350 degrees 10 to 15 minutes until brown around the edges.
- Do not overcook. Remove with spatula to paper towels to cool.
- Makes 24 to 28 cookies.

MOLASSES KRINKLES

1 c. brown sugar
¾ c. shortening
1 egg
3 tbs. molasses
2-¼ c. flour
½ tsp. salt
1-½ tsp. baking soda
1 tsp. cinnamon
½ tsp. ginger
½ tsp. cloves
¼ c. white sugar

- Cream brown sugar and shortening.
- Beat egg. Add to sugar mixture.
- Add molasses. Mix well.
- Mix flour, baking soda and spices together. Add gradually to molasses mixture.
- Form dough into balls about the size of a large walnut. Flour hands if dough is too sticky.
- Press each ball into a small dish of sugar.
- Put each cookie, sugared side up, on an ungreased cookie sheet about 1-½ inches apart.
- Poke an indention in each ball with a finger.
- Drop 2 or 3 drops of water with a spoon or an eye dropper in each indention.
- Bake about 12 minutes in a 350 degree oven until golden.
- Remove with a spatula to cool on paper towels.
- Makes about 30 cookies.

PEANUT BUTTER COOKIES

1 c. brown sugar
1 c. white sugar
1 c. shortening
1 c. chunky peanut butter
½ tsp. salt
2 eggs
2 c. flour
1 tsp. baking soda
1 tsp. vanilla

- Blend sugars and shortening. Add peanut butter. Mix well.
- Beat eggs. Add to mixture. Add vanilla. Mix.
- Mix salt, flour and baking soda and add a little at a time to dough, mixing between each addition.
- Shape into 1-¼ inch diameter balls. Flour hands if dough is to sticky.
- Place balls on an ungreased cookie sheet about 2 inches apart.
- Dip fork in flour and flatten each ball with the fork.
- Bake in a 350 degree oven about 12 minutes. Remove with a spatula to paper towels to cool.
- Makes about 4 doz. cookies.

U.C. BROWNIES

During the late nineteen hundred and twenties, these Brownies were made in a certain bakery on Channing Avenue, close to Sather Gate at the University of California in Berkeley, California. It was a small sweet smelling place where students would stop for snacks. Brownies were our special favorite and it was only after a great deal of cajoling that we obtained the recipe.

Perhaps it is no different than many other good Brownie recipes, but the memory attached makes it special to me and they are good.

> **2 squares bitter chocolate (if unavailable, use unsweeten-**
> **ed chocolate)**
> **¼ c. butter**
> **2 eggs**
> **1 c. sugar**
> **½ c. flour**
> **1 c. chopped walnuts**
> **½ tsp. vanilla**
> **¼ tsp. salt**

- Melt together the chocolate and the butter.
- Beat eggs. Add chocolate mixture to eggs, beating well.
- Add sugar, salt and vanilla. Beat.
- Add flour. Mix well.
- Add nuts.
- Spread thickly on a greased 9 x 9 baking pan.
- Bake for 25 to 30 minutes in a 350 degree oven, until a tester thrust in center comes out clean.
- Cut into squares and remove from pan at once.
- Cool Brownies on a wire rack.
- Makes 16 squares.

APPLE PIE

Flaky Pie Crust dough (see index)
6 to 8 Granny Smith or Pippin apples
1 tsp. ground nutmeg
½ c. sugar

- Using ½ the dough, roll out on a floured board to ¼ inch thick.
- Fit on a greased pie plate, shaping to size and cutting off dough at edges of rim.
- Peel, core and slice apples thin. Place in a bowl. Sprinkle sugar and nutmeg over them , tossing to cover all slices.
- Pour apple slices into uncooked pie shell. Pile the fruit 1 inch or so in a low mound higher than the rim.
- Roll out other half of pie crust dough on board. Place over apples. Cut extended edges to fit, after covering apples completely.
- Flour a fork and press top and bottom edges of dough together, fluting and sealing around the pie.
- Gash the center of top with a knife to allow any gathered steam to escape, while baking.
- Bake in center rack of oven at 375 degrees for 30 minutes. Turn oven to 350 degrees and bake for about 20 to 30 minutes longer, until a fork thrust in center of pie indicates apples are soft.
- Remove from oven and cool on a wire rack.
- Freezes well.

EVERYBODY KNOWS LEMON HEAVEN

1 14 oz. can condensed milk
1 c. sugar
1 pkg. lemon jello
2 or 3 medium lemons
¾ c. water
1 16 oz. box lemon wafers

- Chill can of condensed milk.
- Crush lemon wafers into crumbs to make 2 cups.
- Mix sugar and lemon jello.
- Grate rind of 1 lemon and squeeze lemons to make a generous ¼ c. of juice.
- Add to jello and sugar mixture.
- Boil water and add to jello mixture, stirring until jello and sugar are dissolved.
- Chill in refrigerator until slightly firm, about 20 minutes.
- Whip cold condensed milk in a cold bowl until of a thick creamy texture.
- Fold into chilled jello.
- Line bottom of a buttered 1-½ qt. casserole with ¾ of the crushed wafers.
- Pour jello mixture gently over wafers. Sprinkle rest of wafer crumbs on top.
- Chill thoroughly until set.
- Delicious with whipped cream on top, or just by itself.

FLAKY PIE CRUST

1-½ c. flour
½ tsp. salt
½ c. shortening
⅓ c. cold water, approximately

- Measure flour, salt and shortening into a mixing bowl.
- Cut shortening into bits the size of peas with 2 table knives, cutting crosswise against each other.
- Stir in cold water a little at a time, mixing with a table knife, using a push and pull motion, scraping flour from around the edges of the bowl.
- As dough mixes, add a bit more water until it adheres together and finally forms a ball.
- Avoid touching the dough with warmth of hands while mixing, as this thoughens the dough.
- Turn out onto a floured board.
- Roll with a floured rolling pin to a flat piece about 12 to 14 inches and about ¼ inch thick.
- Fold envelope fashion with a quick touch of the fingers.
- Roll out again until thin enough for a pie crust, about ¼ inch thick.
- Place a sheet of dough large enough to amply cover a greased pie plate, fitting the pan and cutting off the outside edges at the rim.
- If making a covered pie, roll out the rest of the dough for the top.
- If only one crust is needed, either make a shell of the other half of the dough to bake along with your pie; or use the rest of the dough to make Cinnamon Rounds (see index); or just keep remainder wrapped tightly in plastic wrap, to use later. It will keep several days in the refrigerator.
- The baked shell or the Cinnamon Rolls may also be frozen.

FLOATING ISLAND

I'm tempted to say, "It is necessary to have a green glass bowl in which to serve this delectably light dessert." That's just because Mom always served it that way. It was so beautiful. She always brought it in like a crown on a tray and ladled servings with a large silver spoon into individual green glass bowls, each with its own heavenly fluff of an "island" floating on top. Marvelous with Nutmeg Sugar Cookies. (See index.)

> **4 c. milk**
> **4 eggs**
> **1 tsp. vanilla**
> **½ c. sugar**
> **½ tsp. salt**
> **2 rounded tbs. cornstarch**
> **2 tbs. water**
> **Nutmeg to taste**

- Separate eggs.
- Beat yolks. Beat whites separately until stiff.
- Bring 3 c. milk to a simmer in a large pot.
- Do not boil.
- Drop the beaten egg whites by tablespoonsful into the hot milk.
- Simmer 4 minutes, then turn "islands" over with a large slotted spoon to simmer 4 minutes on the other side. Remove floating "islands" gently with the slotted spoon to a colander to drain.
- Slightly cool milk.
- Mix cornstarch with water.
- Pour another cup of milk into beaten egg yolks. Add sugar, salt and vanilla. Beat. Add cornstarch mixed with water. Pour into cooled milk.
- Stir and cook until of a custard consistency, 10 to 15 minutes.
- Pour into large glass serving bowl. Place "islands" on top of custard in bowl.
- Sprinkle nutmeg on each egg white "island."
- Serve at room temperature.
- Serves 6.

GRAHAM CRACKER CRUMB SHELL

1-½ c. graham cracker crumbs
¼ c. sugar
½ tsp. ground cinnamon
½ tsp. ground nutmeg
¼ c. softened butter

- Mix crumbs, sugar, cinnamon and nutmeg well. Add to softened butter and mix well.
- Press into a 9 inch pie plate, covering sides and bottom.
- Bake at 350 degrees for 10 minutes.
- Cool on a wire rack.
- Especially adaptable to Sour Cream Cheese pie (see index).

JAM TARTS

Flaky Pie Crust dough (see index)
Plum, apricot, strawberry jam, or orange marmalade (see index)

- Roll half of the dough to about ¼ inch thin on a floured board.
- Cut into pieces about 4 to 5 inches square. Gather scraps together and reroll for more dough squares.
- Place 2 tbs. jam of your choice in center of each square.
- Fold each over and press and pinch closed at the edges and top, to completely enclose the jam filling.
- Prick with a fork once in center to allow any gathered steam to escape.
- Place tarts on cookie sheet. Bake 20 minutes at 375 degrees until crust is slightly browned and flaky.
- Remove with a spatula to a wire rack to cool.
- One may make half tarts and half Cinnamon Rounds (see index) at the same time, if desired.
- Tarts may be frozen.

ROSEMARY APPLE PUDDING

1 cube butter
6 or 8 Pippin or Granny Smith apples
2 doz. small marshmallows or enough to make one layer in the casserole
½ c. sugar
Cinnamon
¾ c. flour
1 c. brown sugar
¼ pt. cream
Butter to grease casserole

- Peel apples, core and slice thin.
- In a 2 qt. deep buttered casserole, place a layer of the apple slices.
- Sprinkle with sugar and cinnamon. Repeat layers.
- Cover with a layer of marshmallows.
- Add another layer of apple slices, sprinkling a little sugar and cinnamon over them.
- Melt butter and mix with flour and brown sugar.
- Spread over top of layers in casserole.
- Bake in a medium oven, covered, about ½ to ¾ hour, at 350 degrees.
- When apples are soft, uncover and bake 10 minutes longer. Baking time depends upon kind of apples used and their ripeness.
- Serve with whipped cream or ice cream over the top.
- Serves 6 or 8.

WALNUT TORTE

4-½ tbs. soft butter
1-1/8 c. light brown sugar
3 eggs
2-⅔ c. finely ground walnuts
1 tsp. vanilla
1 pint whipping cream
1 tsp. sugar, or to taste
1 box fresh strawberries, or 2 large ripe bananas

- Grind walnuts.
- In a mixing bowl, thoroughly cream butter and brown sugar.
- Separate eggs and beat yolks and whites separately.
- Add beaten egg yolks to creamed mixture, blending well.
- Add ground walnuts and mix well.
- Fold in beaten egg whites.
- Place mixture in 2 buttered cake pans.
- Bake 30 minutes at 350 degrees on center rack of oven. Do not over bake.
- Remove layers from oven and place on wire rack to cool.
- Clean and slice strawberries, or peel and slice bananas.
- Whip cream sweetened with a little sugar and spread over fruit between layers and on top, if desired.

This is an old fashioned dessert and delicious. If using whipped cream is too rich for your taste, Custard Sauce (see index) over the fruit is a fine substitute.

ST. GEORGE HOTEL, VOLCANO, CA.—CIRCA—1862   GLADYS CRUM—1986

SARA'S PEACHY DESSERT

There is a three story hotel in the small town of Volcano, in the Mother Lode country of California. It dates back to the Civil War era. The charm of the place, with its outside balconies entwined with stalwart old vines, emanantes from the building, like the warmth from its native rock fireplace. It has stood there since 1862 and today shows no sign of diminishing its hospitality as an established hostelry.

There are fourteen rooms which are well occupied on occasions by those who love the nostalgia roused by the sight of the steep inner staircase, the huge stone fireplace in the parlour and the antique furnishings throughout. Surrounded by the little town, it stands today as a beautiful and living reminder of those earlier mining days.

Now dinners are served there from Wednesday through Sunday. Sara, the cook, whose personality fits the place like a glove, adds her talents and expertise to the wonderful meals.

Here is one of her special desserts which we enjoyed during the fresh peach season. So deliciously simple.

4 fresh peaches
½ c. brown sugar
½ c. chopped walnuts
2 tbs. melted butter

- Mix the brown sugar, chopped walnuts and melted butter to make a paste.
- Peel, remove the pit and halve the fresh peaches.
- Fill each cavity with the walnut mixture and place the open peaches on a flat pan that will go under the broiler.
- Broil about 3 inches from the flame until sugar melts and bubbles. Watch carefully, as sugar will burn quickly.
- Serve warm, with ice cream on top, if desired.
- Serves 4.

SOUR CREAM CHEESE PIE

Graham Cracker Crumb Pie Shell (see index)
4 3 oz. pkgs., or 1 8 oz. pkg and 1 3 oz. pkg., cream cheese
½ c. sugar
2 eggs
½ tsp. vanilla
¾ c. sour cream
2 tbs. sugar
½ tsp. vanilla

- Beat eggs.
- Whip cheese smooth at room temperature.
- Add sugar, eggs and vanilla.
- Beat 1 minute only at high speed on the electric beater.
- Pour into a graham cracker pie shell. Bake 20 minutes at 350 degrees.
- Remove from oven.
- Mix sour cream, sugar and vanilla and spread on top of warm pie.
- Bake 5 minutes at 350 degrees.
- Remove from oven at once to cool on a wire rack.
- Best made a day before serving. It may be served the same day if chilled well.
- Makes 8 delicious servings.

PICKLES

BREAD AND BUTTER PICKLES
CELERY RELISH
MIXED MUSTARD PICKLES
DILLY STRINGS

PRESERVES

APPLE MARMALADE
APRICOT JAM
CRANBERRY ORANGE CONSERVE
CHUNKY ORANGE MARMALADE
PEACH CONSERVE
PEAR HARLEQUIN
PLUM JAM
SPICED BOSC (WINTER) PEARS

BREAD AND BUTTER PICKLES

10 medium size cucumbers
2-½ c. water
1-½ c. vinegar
1 tsp. salt
3-½ c. vinegar
1 c. water
1-½ c. sugar
1 tsp. celery seed
1 tsp. mustard seed
1 tsp. tumeric

• Cut cucumbers into ¼ inch thick slices. Place in a large stainless steel kettle.
• Add water, 1-½ c. vinegar and salt. Bring to a boil. Stir.
• Remove from heat. Let stand 30 minutes.
• Drain and pack into hot sterilized canning jars.
• Mix 3-½ c. vinegar, water, sugar, celery seed, mustard seeds and tumeric in a small cooking pan.
• Bring to a boil, stirring.
• Pour over cucumber slices in jars to ½ inch of the top.
• Seal at once, while liquid is still hot in jars.
• Makes 8 pints.

CELERY RELISH

2 large bunches of celery
4 large yellow onions
3 large green peppers
1-⅓ c. sugar
3 c. cider vinegar
2 tbs. mustard seed
2 tbs. salt.

- Dice celery.
- Peel and chop onions.
- Remove membranes and seeds and coarsely chop green peppers.
- Combine celery, green peppers, onion, sugar, vinegar, mustard seed and salt. Mix and bring to a boil in a large stainless steel pot.
- Simmer 20 minutes. Stir frequently.
- Pack in hot sterilized jars and seal at once.
- Great on hamburgers.

MIXED MUSTARD PICKLES

1 large head cauliflower
3 large green bell peppers
1 lb. small white onions
2 lbs. green tomatoes (if available)
2 c. small pickling cucumbers, about 1-½ to 2 inches long
5 unpeeled medium cucumbers
4 tbs. salt
8 c. water
3 c. vinegar
2-½ c. sugar
2 tsp. celery seed
2 c. water
¼ c. flour
¾ tsp. tumeric
¼ c. dry mustard

- Cut flowerets from cauliflower and separate into bite size pieces.
- Remove membranes and seeds from peppers and cut into bite size pieces.
- Peel white onions.
- Slice unpeeled medium cucumbers ¼ inch thick, to make 4 cups.
- If green tomatoes are not used, increase amounts of other vegetables as desired.
- Combine all vegetables in a large mixing bowl.
- Blend salt and 4 cups water and pour over vegetables. Let stand overnight. Drain the next day.
- Place vegetables in a large cooking pot. Add 4 c. clear water.
- Bring to a boil. Let cool, then drain.
- Combine vinegar, sugar and celery seed in a saucepan.
- Blend flour, tumeric and mustard in 2 c. water. Stir into vinegar and sugar mixture. Cook until of a gravy-like consistency.
- Pour mustard sacue over vegetables in a large cooking pot and stir carefully to cover all vegetables. Simmer 5 minutes, stirring frequently.
- Fill clean hot pint jars within ¼ inch of the top and seal at once.
- Especially good as an accompaniment for cold meats or ham, in sandwiches, or on a buffet table.
- Makes 8 to 10 pints.

DILLY STRINGS

        4 lbs. green string beans
        4 c. water
        3 c. cider vinegar
        2 tsp. salt
        ⅔ c. sugar
        2 small hot dried red peppers
        4 bay leaves
        6 garlic cloves
        4 medium yellow onions
        8 or 10 large sprigs fresh dill

- Select beans as small and uniform as possible, discarding any that are wilted or broken.
- Wash beans, snap off ends.
- Crush red peppers, discarding seeds.
- Peel and finely chop garlic.
- Peel and thinly slice onions.
- Wash dill sprigs, discarding any heavy stems.
- Combine water, vinegar, salt, sugar, red pepper, bay leaves, garlic and onions in a cooking pot.
- Bring to a boil, then simmer for 10 minutes.
- Boil a large pot of boiling water and salt, drop beans into it, and cook 5 minutes, until the beans are just crisp tender.
- Drain immediately. Place upright and close together in hot sterilized jars, along with a sprig of dill in each.
- Pour the hot vinegar liquid over the beans, filling to within ½ inch of the top.
- Seal at once.
- Makes about 8 to 10 pints.

APPLE MARMALADE

6 lb. red skinned Winesap or Jonathan Apples (12 to 14 apples)
6 lb. sugar (12 cups)
6 c. water
4 medium or 3 large oranges
3 medium or 2 large lemons
3 tsp. ground ginger, or to taste
Paraffin

- Combine sugar and water in a large kettle. Bring to a boil.
- Thinly peel oranges and coarsely chop rind. Squeeze out and retain juice.
- Thinly peel lemons and coarsely chop rind. Squeeze out and retain juice. There should be about ⅓ c. of each.
- Add rinds and juice to simmering syrup. Add ginger.
- Simmer 10 minutes.
- Core unpeeled apples and coarsely shred. Add to simmering syrup.
- Cook about 1-½ hours until fruit becomes well cooked and glazed and marmalade slightly coagulates at bottom of pot. Stir occasionally to prevent sticking.
- Pour into hot clean jars to ½ inch of the top. Seal at once with ¼ inch layer of hot paraffin.
- This is an amber colored marmalade with a delightful zestful flavor.
- Makes 14 to 16 half pints or jelly glasses

Hint: Shredded apples may be kept in a bowl with 2 c. water and juice of a lemon, to deter darkening.

APRICOT JAM

15 to 20 lbs. fresh apricots
10 to 15 lbs. sugar (number of cups depends upon amount
of cups of cut up fruit used)
Paraffin

- Wash apricots, cutting off stem marks and any skin blemishes. Discard seeds.
- Cut fruit into pieces. Place in a large bowl.
- Measure fruit by the cupsful, pressing down slightly on fruit in each cup as measured to make a full cup.
- Place fruit by cupsful in one large kettle, about ½ way to the top, or 2 kettles if necessary.
- Add equal cups of sugar for each cup of fruit in each kettle.
- Cook and stir over low heat until sugar is melted and thoroughly mixed with fruit pieces. Bring to a boil, stirring frequently. Turn to simmer, and cook, stirring occasionally, about 1 hour, or until fruit is soft and jam begins to form glazed bubbles on top and coagulates and gathers on bottom of kettle. Do not allow jam to stick to bottom of pan.
- The length of time depends upon amount of jam cooking.
- Pour into sterilized hot jars within ½ inch of top.
- Melt paraffin and spoon ¼ inch layer over hot jam to seal.
- Let stand to cool.
- Makes 6 to 8 pints of jam, again depending on amount of fruit used.

If you have homemade bread and apricot jam in the house, you'll never lack for something special to serve!

CRANBERRY ORANGE CONSERVE

3 large oranges
1 c. raisins
1 c. hot water
6 c. fresh cranberries
2 c. water
2 c. sugar
Paraffin

- Cut up oranges in very small pieces, including pulp and rind, making sure to remove all seeds.
- Soak raisins in hot water for 10 minutes. Drain.
- Wash and clean cranberries.
- Place cranberries, oranges, sugar and water in a large stainless steel cooking pot.
- Bring to a boil, stirring frequently, then turn to simmer.
- Add softened raisins while simmering.
- Cook until orange pieces are soft and tender, cranberries are popped and cooked, and mixture becomes thick and glazed on top, about ¾ hour.
- Stir often to avoid bottom sticking.
- Spoon into hot clean sterilized jars and seal at once with melted paraffin.
- This is a basic recipe. I usually double the amount of ingredients.
- Do not overcook, as cranberries jell quite easily.
- Makes 4 pints, or 8 jelly glasses.

This cranberry sauce may be used as an accompaniment for hot or cold turkey or chicken and a tablespoonful plopped on top of fruit or chicken salad, or cottage cheese, adds a colorful and piquant touch. Try it also on pork chops cooking in a skillet. After frying, and while covered and simmering, add some cranberry sauce on top of each chop. Baste occasionally. Delicious.

CHUNKY ORANGE MARMALADE

5 oranges
3 large lemons
2 medium grapefruit
Water (number of cups depends upon number of cups of pulp made)
Sugar (number of cups depends upon number of cups of pulp made)
Amount of fruit is basic and may be altered to suit the individual taste and supply on hand
Paraffin

- Grind whole fruit with a coarse blade in a meat grinder, or cut by hand into small pieces. Watch for and remove all seeds.
- Measure mixed pulp by cupsful into a large stainless steel or ceramic bowl.
- Cover pulp in bowl with 3 times as much water.
- Let stand overnight at room temperature.
- The next day, place mixed water and pulp in a large stainless steel pot, or 2 pots.
- Boil hard for 20 minutes. Do not cover.
- Stir frequently.
- Remove from heat and let stand overnight again.
- The third day, add 1 cup sugar for each cup of pulp mixture. Fill cooking pots ½ full.
- Bring to a boil, then simmer about 1 to 1-½ hours, or until mixture becomes thick and bubbles are glazed on top. Stir frequently to avoid sticking on the bottom. (The length of time also depends upon the size of the pots and the amount of their contents.)
- Pour into clean hot sterilized jars to within ½ inch of the top.
- Seal while hot with ¼ inch of melted paraffin.

This is a non mushy chewy marmalade in which one can detect real pieces of fruit. It is delicious stuffed, along with brown sugar and butter, into a baking apple; unforgettable on toasted English muffins or sliced fresh homemade bread. Try also a thick slice of ham baked with brown sugar and chunky marmalade spread over the top before baking.

PEACH CONSERVE

1 large orange
1 large lemon
36 ripe peaches
1-½ tsp. ginger
Sugar, about 12 cups
Paraffin

- Chop orange and lemon fine, including pulp and skin. Remove all seeds.
- Peel and cup up peaches, discarding seeds. There should be about 10 to 12 cups of cut up peaches.
- Mix fruit. Add ginger.
- Measure 1 cup sugar for each full cup of fruit.
- Mix well in a large pot. Use 2 pots if necessary, filling each pot about ½ full, to allow for boiling.
- Bring to a boil, stirring frequently, then reduce to a simmer, cooking until mixture becomes thick and bubbles are slightly glazed on top, about 1 hour or longer.
- Pour into hot clean jars or glasses to within ½ inch of top.
- Seal while still hot with ¼ inch melted paraffin.
- Makes 12 to 14 glasses.

PEAR HARLEQUIN

4 lbs. ripe yellow pears
1 16 oz. can crushed pineapple
2 large oranges
1 large lemon
8 c. sugar
1 16 oz. jar Maraschino cherries
Paraffin

- Wash and core pears. Cut into small pieces to make about 8 cups.
- Slice oranges and lemon very thin, including skin, pulp and juice.
- Cut slices in half if too large.
- Drain cherries, saving juice.
- Cut up cherries, to make ½ cup.
- Mix lemon, oranges, pears and about 1-½ cups crushed pineapple, including juice, in a large bowl.
- Measure combined fruits by the cup.
- Add sugar, measuring ¾ cup sugar for each cup fruit pulp.
- Cook in a large cooking pot until thick and amber colored for about ¾ hour. Stir frequently, to prevent sticking.
- Cooking time will vary with amount of fruit used and size of pot.
- Add cherries with their juice and cook 15 minutes longer.
- Pour into clean hot jars or glasses to within ½ inch of top.
- Seal while hot with ¼ inch melted paraffin.
- Makes 8 to 10 glasses or 4 to 5 pints of conserve.

PLUM JAM

15 lbs. plums (reddish purple-meat plums are best for jam)
12 cups sugar (exact number of cups depends upon
number of cups of strained pulp — One cup of pulp to
one cup of sugar)
Paraffin

- Wash and cut plums into pieces, including seeds and skin.
- Cook in a large pot for about ¾ of an hour until pulp is soft enough to be forced through a colander.
- Strain plum pulp into a bowl, discarding skin and seeds left in colander.
- Measure 1 cup sugar for each 1 cup plum pulp into a large cooking pot.
- Cook, stirring, to a boil, then simmer until jam is thick and bubbles on top are glazed and jam begins to coagulate on the bottom of the pot.
- Exact timing depends on amount of pulp used. It should take about ¾ hour.
- Pour into hot sterilized glasses or pint jars to ½ inch of the top.
- Seal while hot with ¼ inch of melted paraffin.
- Makes about 16 glasses or 8 pints of jam.

SPICED BOSC (WINTER) PEARS

6 lbs. pears
10 c. water
5 c. sugar
10 whole cloves
6 bay leaves
Few drops red or green food coloring (optional)

- Wash, halve, quarter and core pears. Do not peel. Keep quarters in a bowl of cold water to deter darkening.
- Mix sugar and water in a large cooking pot. Add cloves and bay leaves.
- Bring to a boil. Turn to simmer and cook for about 10 minutes until sugar is thoroughy dissolved and spices are assimilated into the syrup.
- Add food coloring, enough to give a pleasing red or green color to the syrup. (3 or 4 drops will do.) (Optional.)
- Take pears out of water and drop into simmering syrup. cook until fork-tender, but not soft, about 15 minutes.
- Place pears in hot clean pint jars, packing verticallly as much as possible. Add a bay leaf and clove where possible.
- Pour syrup over pears, keeping it and fruit ¼ inch below top of the jar.
- Seal at once.
- Make about 6 pints.

These make a beautiful salad with a shredded lettuce base and pimento cream cheese balls placed on top of each pear piece. Mix a little of the syrup with mayonnaise for the dressing. Great also as a ham dinner accompaniment, or served in their own juice as dessert, with cookies.

MISCELLANEOUS

OLD FASHIONED NOODLE RING
HOBOS
WELSH RAREBIT

OLD FASHIONED NOODLE RING

3 tbs. butter
¾ c. fine dry bread crumbs
6 oz. fine noodles
3 sprigs parsley
1 egg
½ tsp. salt
¼ tsp. pepper
2 tbs. melted butter

- Chop parsley flowerets to make about 3 tbs. Discard stems.
- Melt butter in a ring pan to cover bottom and sides, or in a regular square baking pan 9 x 9 x 2-½ inches, if ring pan is not available.
- Sprinkle crumbs over the melted butter in pan.
- Cook noodles until tender but not soft, 6 to 8 minutes. Drain under cold water. Place in a bowl. Add melted butter and chopped parsley.
- Beat eggs and mix with salt and pepper. Add to noodles.
- Mix gently and arrange in the buttered pan. Set in a pan of cold water to prevent sticking.
- Bake at 350 degrees for 20 to 30 minutes until eggs are set.
- Unmold, if in a ring pan. Serve with creamed mixture in center.
- Or cut in squares, if in a square pan, and serve creamed mixture on top.
- Great with creamed tuna, chicken or chipped beef.

HOBOS

4 eggs
4 slices bacon
3 medium White Rose potatoes
1 small green pepper
½ tsp. salt
¼ tsp. pepper
1 small yellow onion

- Peel and cook potatoes until firm tender. Coarsely chop to make about 1 cup.
- Cut bacon in ¼ inch pieces crosswise. Fry in a large skillet until crisp tender. Remove bacon pieces from pan. Pour off all grease except about 2 tbs. Save rest of grease for other uses.
- Wash green pepper and remove membranes and seeds. Chop fine to make about 3 tbs.
- Peel and finely chop onion.
- Saute onion and green pepper in bacon grease about 5 minutes until firm tender.
- Add potatoes and bacon. Stir over low heat until well mixed.
- Salt and pepper to taste.
- Beat eggs and pour over potato mixture. Cook over medium heat, stirring gently until eggs are well scrambled.
- Serves 2 generously.

WELSH RAREBIT

2 tbs. butter
2 tbs. flour
1 c. beer
1-½ lb. sharp Cheddar cheese
2 eggs
½ tsp. dry mustard
1 tbs. Worcestershire sauce
½ tsp. salt
¼ tsp. pepper
Crab leg meat sections and/or crab meat optional, about
½ lb. or more
French bread

- Coarsely grate cheese to make about 2 cups.
- Beat eggs well.
- Melt butter in a large skillet.
- Add flour. Slowly stir in the beer. When mixture is thickened and smooth, add the cheese.
- Continue to stir over low heat until cheese is melted.
- Add eggs slowly, stirring until the eggs thicken but do not overcook.
- Add Worcestershire and salt and pepper to taste.
- Place 2 tbs. crab meat or 2 or 3 crab leg meat sections on each piece of toast.
- Pour Rarebit over all immediately and serve at once on heated plates.
- Makes 4 servings.

AND THEN THERE IS ME!

ABOUT MENUS

The menu is a detailed plan of the foods to be served at a meal. The coordination of the courses is the happy objective of the cook, but the preparation of well cooked food is only half the process. The presentation is the other half. The meal should flow from course to course like a well composed song. The foods should be colorful, their aromas setting the mood for the gastronomic pleasures set before the eager guests.

Taste is the prime objective, but tasty food offered in a sloppy manner becomes unattractive and actually less palatable. The creator must not only balance the contents of the meal as to amounts of protein, starch, spice and sweet and sour accents, but also as to color and texture as well. These combinations set the pace for the dinner. Each one becomes a foil for, while blending with, the others. For example, it would be inadvisable to offer a creamed vegetable with a creamed entree, or a fish salad with a fish dinner, or heavy appetizers with a meat entree. Think of a light dessert after a heavy meal, or an eye-filling pie or heavenly cake after a light meal.

There is nothing more disturbing than a nervous hovering cook. Try to plan your dinner so that you will have most things prepared and ready to cook or serve ahead of time. Choose your menu to fit the tastes of your guests. Cook appropriately, although not necessarily to your own ultimate preference. (I've found that I am able to prepare food more easily when looking forward to the final product myself!)

Arrange the centerpiece on the table low enough so that everyone is able to see over it. Conversation is a pleasant addition (although not necessary) to the consumption and enjoyment of a meal and is interrrupted by a distrubing and towering centerpiece.

Finally, avoid overeagerness and enthusiasm for your own creations. Let them speak for themselves. They will be manifested through the glow and satisfaction shown by those gathered around your table.

AND THEN THERE IS ME!

RANDOM DINNER MENUS

Each menu contains a suggested appetizer, salad, entree with vegetable and starch accompaniment and dessert.

The choice of breads, jams, beverages rests on your individual requirements. All recipes, of course, may be interchanged, deleted, or added to at will. Your ingenuity will do the final composing of your menu into a personalized offering.

Good cooking!

(Mark "X" indicates recipe may be found in Recipe Index.)

ROUND STEAK ROLLS (ROULADIN)

Deviled Ham Tarts	X
Celery Victor	X
Rouladin	X
Candied Carrots	X
Parsley Potatoes	X
Applesauce Cake	X

BEEF CURRY (See complete dinner menu on pages 112 through 120)

"HONEY-DO" STEAK

Glad's Clam Dip	X
Applesauce and Raspberry Salad	X
"Honey-Do" Steak	X
Potato Stix	X
Cherry Popper Tomatoes	X
Apple Pie with Cinnamon Sauce	X

MUSHROOM STEAKS FOR TWO

Ham and Liver Pate	X
Fruit Salad	
Mushroom Steaks for Two	X
Corn Souffle	X
Green Beans	
Floating Island	X
Molasses Krinkles	X

RANDOM DINNER MENUS (continued)

BRAISED PICKLED BEEF POT ROAST (SAUERBRATEN)

Kept Cheese and crackers	X
Seven-Up Salad	X
Braised Pickled Beef Pot Roast	X
Wide Noodles	
Nutmeg Carrots	X
Sara's Peachy Dessert	X
Peanut Butter Cookies	X

COUNTRY STYLE PORK RIBS

Tuna Balls	X
Applesauce and Raspberry Salad	X
County Style Pork Ribs	X
Parsley Potatoes	X
Fried Eggplant Slices	X
Maple Mousse	X
Chewy Nut Cookies	X

PENNSYLVANIA POT ROAST

Kept Cheese	X
Crab Cocktail	X
Pennsylvania Pot Roast	X
Honey Glazed Onions	X
Butter or Lima Beans	
Baked Potatoes	
Mom's Fruit Cake	X

OVEN BAKED LAMB CHOPS

Sardine pate	X
Avocado with jellied broth	X
Oven Baked Lamb Chops (with potatoes)	X
Mint Jelly	
Peas	
Apricot Coconut Squares	X

AND THEN THERE IS ME!

RANDOM DINNER MENUS (continued)

VEAL CUTLETS

Crab Delight Dip	X
Parsley Salad	X
Veal Cutlets	X
Sauteed Turnips	X
Creamed Small New Potatoes	
Chews With Whipped Cream	X

SHRIMP SOUFFLE

Spinach Squares	X
Fruit Cooler	X
Banana Nut Bread	X
Shrimp Souffle	X
Broccoli	
Butterscoth Sauce on Ice Cream	X
Nutmeg Sugar Cookies	X

CHICKEN CACCIATORI

Kept Cheese	X
California Cole Slaw	X
Chicken Cacciatori	X
Rice	
Sprouts	
Hot Milk Cake	X

CRAB ENCHILADAS

Celery Root Dip	X
Guacamole Spears	X
Crab Enchiladas	X
Corn Souffle	X
Fried Zucchini	
Lime Sherbet	
Jam Cookies	X

RANDOM DINNER MENUS (continued)

CHILI MEAT LOAF

Newt's Favorite Cheese Rounds	X
Spinach Salad	X
Campfire Chili over Chile Meat Loaf	X
String Beans	
Floating Island	X
Nutmeg Sugar Cookies	X

FIESTA CHICKEN

Marinated Sprouts and Mushrooms	X
Nogales Salad	X
Fiesta Chicken	X
Broccoli	
Lemon Souffle Pie	X

Don't forget HAM AND LAMB STEW (Wuddlemousse) (X) with ONE-TWO-THREE BREAD (Eins-Zwei-Drei Brot) (X) and WINE JELLO (X) on Christmas Eve!

INDEX OF RECIPES
(First number is Section. Second number is Page.)
(Example: 3/125)

APPETIZERS

avocado appetizer, 3/125
celery root dip, 3/126
cheese rounds, newt's favorite, 3/144
cheese, kept, 3/136
chutney dip, 3/158
clam dip, glad's, 3/134
crab dip, delight, 3/130
crab cocktail, 3/129
croutons, 3/131
dipping sauce, 3/133
deviled ham tarts, 3/132
meat balls, cocktail, 3/128
mushrooms, stuffed, 3/138
pork, chinese dunking, 3/127
queso caliente dip, 3/250
sardine pate, 3/141
scallops ceviche, 3/139
shrimp cocktail, 3/140
spinach cheese squares, 3/142
sprouts and mushrooms, marinated, 3/137
sprouts and water chestnuts,
marinated, 3/143
tuna balls, judy's, 3/145

BREADS

banana nut, 1/296
bowls, crust, 1/29
cinnamon buns, 1/28
crisps, poppy seed, 3/298
one-two-three bread, 1/26-27
pizza, thick crust, 2/82
stix, flaky, 3/297

CAKES

applesauce, 3/277
coffee, 1/31
cranberry, inverted, 3/280
fruit, 1/32
fruitcake, poor man's, 2/105
fried cakes, 1/33
frosting, mocha, 3/278

INDEX OF RECIPES (continued)

CAKES (continued)

golden pound, 2/103
hot milk, with coconut topping, 3/279
old reliable, raisin, 1/34
pineapple, upside down, 2/104
prince of wales, 2/106
spanish bun, 3/281
white fruit, 3/282

COOKIES

apricot coconut squares, 3/305
cinnamon rounds, 3/163
chews, 3/306
chocolate coconut kisses, 3/308
danish jam, 3/309
dainty butter, 2/108
molasses krinkles, 3/310
nutmeg sugar, 1/35
peanut butter, 3/311
u.c. brownies, 3/312
walnut snaps, 3/307

DESSERTS

bananas, fried, 3/162
crumb shell, graham cracker, 3/317
floating island, 3/316
jello, wine, 2/112
lemon heaven, everybody knows, 3/314
mousse, maple, 2/111
peachy dessert, sara's, 3/323
pie, apple, 3/313
pie crust, flaky, 3/315
pie, lemon souffle, 2/210
pie, sour cream cheese, 3/324
pudding, apricot bread, 1/44
pudding, carrot, 2/109
pudding, old fashioned rice, 1/45
pudding, red tapioca, 1/46
pudding, rosemary apple, 3/319
tarts, jam, 3/318
torte, walnut, 3/320

FISH

clam or crab fritters, 3/213
clam sauce with bacon, over
spaghetti, 2/81
codfish casserole with crouton
topping, 3/88
crab stuffed bell peppers, 3/214
crab cakes, chinese, 2/73
crab enchiladas, san francisco
special, 2/86
crab enchiladas, southwestern, 3/240
crab quiche, 2/87
crab meat sauce with swiss cheese
pie, 3/221
crab rarebit, san francisco, 2/90
halibut slices, baked, 3/212
hangtown fry, 3/217
salmon cakes, 3/209
salmon, overnight casserole, 3/219
salmon quiche, 3/222
shrimp, curried sauce in avocado, 3/210
shrimp, curried casserole with rice, 2/89
shrimp, no-fail souffle, 3/218
shrimp sambal, 3/161
shrimp sauce with parsley, in
avocado, 3/211
trout fillets, 3/225

MEATS

BEEF

brisket, german style, 1/9
cabbage rolls, old country, 1/12
chili, california campfire, 3/235
chimichangas, 3/239
curry, beef, 3/159
   (see curry dinner for six, 3/155-163)
joe's special, 2/61
meat balls, sweet and sour, 2/64
meat loaf, chili, 3/236
meat loaf, old fashioned, 3/62
meat patties, 1/10
pot roast, braised, pickled, 1/8
pot roast, mexican, 3/247
round steak, "honey-do", 3/170
round steak, rolls, 1/14

MEATS (continued)

BEEF (continued)

    short ribs, 2/63
    steak, green pepper, 3/166
    steak, mushroom, for two, 3/171
    steak, parmesan, 2/66
    steak, san luis obispo, 3/180
    stew, rodeo, 3/178
    stew, siempre, with biscuit topping, 3/179
    tacos, corn chip (sombreros), 3/238
    yum yum balls, 2/65

HAM

    ham and lamb stew, 1/11
    ham and scalloped potatoes, 3/168
    ham and sweet potato casserole, 3/169
    ham and cheese tarts, 3/167

LAMB

    chops, compass rose, 3/147
    chops, oven baked, 3/173

LIVER

    liver and onion, ole, 3/246
    liver, oriental beef, 2/76
    liver, parsley lemon, 3/174

PORK

    chops, and apple casserole, 1/13
    chops, florentine, 3/176
    chops, old farm, 3/172
    chops, smoked, curried, 3/151
    cranberry, 3/150
    kabobs, chinese, barbecued, 2/18
    mandarin, 2/75
    pot roast, with sauerkraut, 1/16
    ribs, country style, 3/149
    roast, pennsylvania, 3/175
    spareribs, eugene oven baked, 3/165
    steaks and parsnips, 3/177

INDEX OF RECIPES (continued)

MEATS (continued)

SAUSAGE

sausage with sauerkraut, 1/15

VEAL

cutlets, 1/17
italiano, 2/83
palazza, 2/84

PICKLES

bread and butter, 3/326
celery relish, 3/327
dilly strings, 3/329
mixed mustard, 3/328

PRESERVES

apple butter, 1/40
apple marmalade, 3/330
apricot jam, 3/331
cranberry orange conserve, 3/332
lemon butter, 1/42
orange marmalade, chunky, 3/333
peach conserve, 3/334
pear harlequin, 3/335
pears, spiced bosc (winter), 3/337
plum jam, 3/336

POULTRY

CHICKEN

cacciatori, 2/79
croquettes, baked, 3/182
drumsticks, chinese barbecued, 2/72
drumsticks, dijon broiled, 3/183
easy baked, 3/184
enchiladas, creamed style, 3/241
fiesta, 3/242
tostada de pollo (chicken tostadas), 3/253
thighs, easy fixin' mexican, 3/237
wings, oriental, 2/71

POULTRY (continued)

TURKEY

"so long" turkey, 3/185

SALADS

applesauce raspberry, 3/256
avocado in jellied broth, 3/255
baby sea shell, 3/257
celery victor, 2/98
cucumbers, sour cream, 3/266
chicken, glad's special, 3/260
cole slaw, california, 3/258
eggs, stuffed, 2/96
jicama, 3/261
nogales, 3/248
palace court, 2/95
parsley, so easy, 3/267
pearl onion, 3/262
potato, german, 3/259
sauerkraut, 3/263
seven up, applesauce, 3/264
shrimp curry, 3/265
spears, guacamole, 3/244
spinach, 3/268
strips, roquefort, 2/97

SALAD DRESSINGS

court louis, 2/99
mom's, 3/269
old fashioned, boiled, 2/100
roquefort cheese, tangy, 3/271
spinach, 3/270
victor, 2/101

SOUPS

clam chowder, sacramento, 3/273
lima bean, 3/274
vichyssoise, 3/275

SAUCES

butterscotch, 3/284
chili, glad's, 3/287

SAUCES (continued)

cinnamon, hot, 3/288
curry, 3/285
custard, 1/37
dipping, 3/94
guacamole, indispensable, 3/245
hard, 1/38
hollandaise, sara's mock, 3/291
huevos rancheros sauce, carmelita, 3/232
lemon, 3/290
marinade, special steak, 3/292
meat sauce, italian, 2/80
mustard, for ham, 3/289
salsa, fresh, 3/243
soft, 1/39
spaghetti sauce, 3/286
sprightly, 3/293
sweet and sour, 2/77
tomato, thick and tangy, 3/294

SANDWICHES

crab melt, 3/289
corned beef, 49'er, 3/300
home style monte cristo, 3/301
mushroom and swiss cheese on rye, 3/302
piquant shrimp rolls, 3/303

VEGETABLES

beans, basic, all purpose, 3/233
beans, barbecued, mixed, 3/187
beans, black, chili, 3/234
beans, green, with sweet and sour sauce
and bacon, 1/20
beans, refried, 3/251
cabbage, red, 1/21
chili rellenos, oven, 3/249
cauliflower, smokey, au gratin, 3/203
carrots, candied, 3/188
carrots, nutmeg, 3/197
carrots, rhineland style, 1/19
corn fritters, 3/190
corn souffle, 3/191
eggplant, slices, fried, 3/192
hominy, gypsy, 3/194
onions, honey glazed, 3/195

INDEX OF RECIPES (continued)

VEGETABLES (continued)

onions, sweet red rose, 3/205
onions, tangy red rose, 3/206
peppers, bell, glad's stuffed, 3/164
pepper, bell and red onions,
sauteed, 3/201
potato pancakes, 1/22
potatoes, parsley, 3/198
potato stix, 3/199
rice, or mashed potato fritters, 3/200
sauerkraut, 1/23
sauerkraut, with apples, 1/24
sweet potato balls, 3/204
tomatoes, broiled, especially good, 3/193
tomatoes, cherry popper, 3/189
turnips, sauteed, 3/202
yam pancakes, 3/207
zucchini, souffle, 3/208
zucchini, tossed, 3/196

MISCELLANEOUS

apples, country fried, 1/50
cheese, cottage, 1/49
cheese enchiladas, southwestern, 3/252
doughnuts, danish, 1/51
fruit cooler, 3/116
huevos rancheros, carmelitos, 3/231
hobos, 3/340
noodle ring, old fashioned, 3/339
pancakes, sunday morning, 2/107
rarebit, welsh, 3/341
walnuts, candied, 2/113

JUST IN THE NICK OF TIME

(How could I have almost forgotten these? The "urgency" of Press Time brought them quickly to mind.)

artichokes florentine, 3/361
contigo stew, 3/359
custard layer cake (boston cream
pie), 3/363
lemon chicken, 3/362
ravioli with shrimp sauce, 3/360

"Contigo"

CONTIGO STEW

"Contigo" translated, means "With You." It recalls many happy days on our old, restored, 40 foot fish boat; outfitted with a wide working deck, a crow's nest for a fish lookout, a cozy forward cabin with bunks and a tiny galley.

Anchored in the harbor at Catalina Island, off the Southern California coast, we often had visitors arriving by dinghy, who invariably tied up along-side, climbed aboard and remained for a "Bite."

Limited by space and availability, Contigo Stew was concocted with ingredients on hand and a bit of loving care and enthusiasm. Accompanied by "Bisquick" biscuits, it became a Standby Stew, ready and hot in a comparatively short time.

It may not look as attractive, ladled into bowls when served in more conventional surroundings. However, it is still a most satisfying and filling dish. Proportions and quantities are adjusted to supplies on board and the size of the hungry hoard!

**Left-over well done beef
1 12 oz. can corned beef
2 14 oz. cans golden hominy
2 tbs. bacon grease
2 large yellow onions
1 green Bell pepper
3 or 4 stalks celery
2 beef bouillon cubes
1 c. hot water
1 8 oz. can tomato sauce
1 4 oz. can sliced mushrooms
1 tsp. garlic salt
2 tsp. chile powder, or to taste
1 c. water
¾ c. dry red wine**

- Shred beef.
- Shred corned beef.
- Peel and chop onions.
- Remove membranes and seeds from Bell pepper. Chop.
- Chop celery.
- In a large skillet, saute onion, green pepper and celery in bacon grease until limp.
- Add cooked beef and corned beef. Stir.
- Add tomato sauce, tomatoes, mushrooms, hominy, chile powder and garlic salt.
- Mix well.
- Add bouillon cubes dissolved in hot water and ¾ c. red wine.
- Simmer at least 15 minutes, or longer, until time to serve.
- Good with hot biscuits and honey.
- Serves 6 to 10 (or whatever).

RAVIOLI WITH SHRIMP SAUCE

24 large fresh spinach ravioli
About 8 c. water
1 tsp. salt
4 oz. cream cheese
2 tbs. butter
½ tsp. pepper
½ tsp. garlic salt
½ c. half and half cream
¾ lb. medium size cooked shrimp
1 large lemon
Parmesan cheese

- Squeeze lemon to make 1-½ tsp.
- Drop ravioli one by one into salted boiling water, allowing them to dance freely.
- Boil until all ravioli rise to the top and are firm tender and unbroken, about 10 minutes. (To test tenderness, pierce with a fork.)
- Drain, pouring ravioli carefully into a colander.
- In a heavy skillet, melt butter, cream cheese and garlic salt until smooth and well blended. Add half and half and heat well. Do not boil.
- Drop the cooked shrimp into the sauce. Slowly add lemon juice and pepper.
- Stir carefully to mix.
- Toss ravioli into shrimp sauce and serve with Parmesan cheese, Italian bread and a green salad with Italian dressing.
- Serves 4 (6 ravioli for each person).

ARTICHOKES FLORENTINE

12 medium to large artichokes
1 tsp. salt
2 pkgs. frozen chopped spinach
4 tbs. flour
1 tsp. seasoned salt
6 or 8 fresh mushrooms

1 egg
½ c. dry bread crumbs
4 tbs. butter
Parmesan cheese
Florentine sauce (see below)

- Remove leaves from raw artichokes. Trim bottom hearts of blemishes.
- Boil hearts in salted water until fork tender, about 20 to 30 minutes.
- Drain. Cool. Cut out choke from each artichoke bottom center, with a sharp knife or a spoon and discard.
- Cook chopped spinach according to package directions. Drain well.
- Wash, pat dry and chop mushrooms.
- Beat egg.
- Roll artichoke bottoms in flour, then in beaten egg and then in dry bread crumbs, coating well.
- Saute in butter until golden brown.
- Fill each artichoke bottom with cooked spinach. Arrange in a shallow baking dish.
- Cover with 2 cups Florentine sauce. Sprinkle with Parmesan cheese.
- Bake in a 375 degree oven until brown, about 10 minutes.
- Serve as a vegetable with hot beef or ham dinners, or as an appetizer, at room temperature.
- Serves 6.

FLORENTINE SAUCE

3 tbs. butter
5 tbs. flour
2 c. milk
Salt and pepper to taste
¾ cup Gruyere cheese

- Melt butter in medium skillet. Do not let it brown.
- Add flour all at once. Stir and cook until pale gold.
- Remove from heat.
- Add milk all at once.
- Return to heat. Cook and stir until thick adding salt and pepper to taste.
- Add Gruyere cheese. Stir until cheese melts.

LEMON CHICKEN

2 cut up fryers
2 large lemons
⅓ c. flour
1-½ tsp. salt
½ tsp. paprika
4 tbs. salad oil
3 tbs. brown sugar
1 c. chicken broth
3 or 4 sprigs fresh mint or 3 tsp. dried mint leaves

- Grate peel from 1 lemon. Squeeze juice over chicken pieces.
- Shake chicken pieces in a bag with flour, salt and paprika.
- Brown chicken in a large skillet until golden brown on all sides, about 10 minutes. Arrange browned pieces in a large casserole.
- Sprinkle grated lemon peel over pieces.
- Slice other lemon and arrange slices over chicken.
- Sprinkle brown sugar over pieces.
- Pour in chicken broth.
- Sprinkle mint on top.
- Cover and bake at 325 degrees until chicken is tender, about 35 to 45 minutes.
- Baste chicken with pan juices occasionally.
- Serve with mashed potatoes and a green vegetable.
- Serves 6 to 8.

CUSTARD FILLED SPONGE LAYER CAKE
(Boston Cream Pie)

TO MAKE SPONGE LAYERS

3 eggs   1 tsp. baking powder
1 c. sugar   ¼ tsp. salt
3 tbs. water   1 tsp. each, lemon flavor and vanilla
1 c. flour

- Mix flour, baking powder and salt in a separate bowl.
- Beat eggs well, preferably with an electric beater.
- Add sugar. Beat.
- Add water. Continue to beat.
- Add dry ingredients. Continue to beat.
- Add flavorings last. Beat.
- Pour into 2 greased layer cake pans and bake at 375 degrees about 20 minutes or until tester thrust in center comes out clean. Bubbles will form in layers as they bake.
- Handle carefully so that sponge layers do not fall.

CUSTARD FILLING

2 5 oz. cans evaporated milk   1 tbs. cornstarch
1 egg   2 tbs. water
Pinch of salt   1 tsp. vanilla
½ c. sugar

- Add equal parts of water to evaporated milk in a double boiler.
- Beat egg. Add to cream, along with sugar and salt. Stir well.
- Add vanilla and cornstarch thinned with water.
- Cook in a double boiler, stirring until of custard consistency, about 8 minutes. Cool. Spread on bottom layer of cake placed on a cake plate. Top with other layer.

ICING

⅓ c. butter
2 c. powdered sugar
1 egg
2 tsp. cocoa or powdered chocolate

- Cream butter and sugar. Add cocoa. Mix well.
- Separate egg and beat yolk and white separately.
- Add beaten yolk to creamed mixture.
- Fold in beaten white. Cream.
- Spread on top layer only.
- Serve at room temperature.

"Glad, while you're up, may I have some more-----?"

"Lots Of Goodies Are Waiting At The End Of The Road
To Grandma's And Grandpa's House"

365